THE BOOK OF AYLESBURY

COVER: Vale of Aylesbury Steeple Chase, from a painting by F. C. Turner
engraved by C. & G. Hunt in 1836.

Aylesbury a century ago. (County Museum)

THE BOOK OF
AYLESBURY

AN HISTORICAL ANTHOLOGY
IN PICTURES

BY

CLIVE BIRCH FSA FRSA

BARON
MCMXCIV

ORIGINALLY PUBLISHED BY BARRACUDA BOOKS IN 1975,
IN A REVISED EDITION IN 1984 AND IN THIS
THIRD EDITION BY BARON BIRCH FOR QUOTES LIMITED IN 1993

PRODUCED BY KEY COMPOSITION, CHENEY & SONS,
HILLMAN PRINTERS (FROME) AND WBC BOOKBINDERS

ISBN 0 86023 543 2

Contents

Acknowledgements

The Book of Aylesbury owes much to many; to all those people who gave encouragement, support, information, advice and material help, my thanks.

In particular, I am grateful for the guidance and knowledge of the late Hayward Parrott, past chronicler of the town, and for access to his collection of memorabilia; for the expert opinion of Mike Farley of the County Museum; for the loan of extensive material by Margaret Sale and Ralph May, and especially for Miss Sale's original print used for the cover design; and to the Osterfield family for the opportunity to delve into the quite remarkable collection of the late Geo. A. Osterfield.

My thanks go too to Christopher Gowing of the County Museum for advice, and help with photographic material and to Rosemary Ewles of the Museum for her help and time; to Elizabeth Elvey and the Buckinghamshire Archaeological Society for their expertise and access to their muniments; to E. J. Davis and Hugh Hanley of the County Record Office for suggestions and much patience in providing information and original material; to Colin Rippon, and the staff of the Reference and Lending Libraries at County Hall for material.

I owe a particular debt of gratitude to two past historians, without whose researches and observations this book would be the poorer: Robert Gibbs and J. K. Fowler.

Formal acknowledgements are also due to the following: reproductions of Crown copyright records in the Public Record Office, by permission of the Controller of HM Stationery Office: to the Trustees of the British Museum; to the Mansell Collection; to Worcestershire Records Office.

For virtually every photographic reproduction, I am indebted more than I can say to my friend and colleague, John Armistead, without whose forbearance, eye for detail and professionalism there would be no illustrations in this book. It is pleasing to record my daughter Emma's help with tables and index.

Note to the Third Edition

I remain grateful to Hugh Hanley of the County Record Office, John Guest, lately of Aylesbury Vale District Council and Rev John Morrison, Vicar of St Mary's for advising on the previous edition.

I am also greatly indebted to Mike Farley of the County Museum for his helpful comments towards revision then and now. My thanks also include various correspondents who have corrected minor errors, John Armistead for 1984 pictures, Alan Knox of County Museum for 1993 material and Bernard Quorrol, Aylesbury's Chief Executive and his staff, especially Teresa Lake, for their help with 'modern' Aylesbury. The Transactions of the Archaeological and Records Societies have yielded helpful facts.

Much of the original work towards this book was done in the old Museum building; it is therefore fitting that it should once more appear, as that building undergoes a massive repair and refit, to house the county's past in glory.

Foreword

Both before and since it became the county town, Aylesbury has been the scene of innumerable important Buckinghamshire occasions. As John Hampden's statue bears witness in the Market Square, the attitude of its citizens has always been robust and independent, politically wayward and socially unpredictable.

Since the last war Aylesbury has lost much—its assize status, its principal hotel, its main line connection, many of its quainter buildings—but it has grown mightily in size and influence, and the dominance of the County Offices rather than the spire of St Mary's Church has not destroyed its setting in its beautiful Vale, with gracious Hartwell to the West, and the escarpments of the Chilterns to which to lift the eyes.

I hope this book will make available to posterity records of past beauty and a determination to conserve what remains in this busy metropolis of Buckinghamshire.

CLAYDON HOUSE
June 1975

Preface

The late Mr Robert Gibbs, FSA, of Aylesbury, published his monumental History of Aylesbury in 1885. No other complete history of the county town has appeared since then, although an attempt was made in 1952 to collate for easy reference a record of the principal changes and outstanding events that had occurred in the previous seventy years.

So The Book of Aylesbury which has been compiled by Mr Clive Birch who has written the text and illustrated it with a wealth of photographs not only of places and events but also of documents bearing upon the town's history and ephemera touching on the social aspect of life in a market and county town in past times, is a welcome and timely arrival in view of the scale of development which has taken place within the last twenty years.

Mr Birch is to be congratulated on the hard work which he has put into his book, coupled with perseverance against odds which at times may have appeared formidable. Not only has he located and examined illustrative material stored in county files and official muniment rooms as well as in private hands, but what is often more difficult, he has succeeded in borrowing much of it for copying and selection, in face of the natural reluctance of owners to lend their material for this purpose.

I hope that The Book of Aylesbury will attain the success which it deserves.

AYLESBURY
June, 1975

The Vale of Aylesbury

Know ye the land where the butter's so yellow,
So rich in its flavour, so sweet to the taste—
Where the milk is so white, where the cream is so mellow—
Ah! sweeter than nectar and thicker than paste?
Know ye the land where the dear little duck
Doth dabble about in the mud and the muck—
Where the little lambs frisk, as bright Phoebus peeps out,
And cock up their tails as they scamper about—
Where the hens, unlike London hens, play not such tricks
As to lay new-laid eggs that contain little chicks—
Where the pasture's so rich, and the cattle so plump,
And milk may be had without using the pump—
Where the voice of the guinea-fowl never is mute,
And each little boy has a whistle or flute—
Where the maidens are soft as the butter they churn,
But the men ar'n't content with the wages they earn—
Where altho' agitators have tried to make head,
And to gull honest Hodge of his dearly earned bread,
And the Arch one himself has endeavoured to spout,
He has found it 'no go' and has had to 'get out'—
Where the night's not disturbed by the nightingale's lay,
For the little boys take all their nesties away—
Where the light wings of Zephyr, when beans are in bloom,
Wax faint while the Thame poureth forth her perfume?
'Tis the Vale, 'tis the Vale, 'tis the far famous Vale,
Near Aylesbury town—within sight of the gaol—
The pride and the boast of the County of Bucks,
That garden of plenty, of pigstyes and ducks,
That Eden on earth, that spot ever sunny,
That place of all places for making of money,
Which floweth with milk and with butter—not honey?

Extract from The Phantom Hound: A Legend of the
Vale of Aylesbury by Frank Percy, 1880.

A Civil Town

In the first place, Aylesbury was nothing but a knoll at the foot of the Chiltern escarpment, looking over a marshy, misty plain. Probably concealed beneath a tangled growth of scrub and trees, it would not have been noticeable to early man half a million years ago, as he flaked flints and scraped the hilltops above for a scant living.

Today Aylesbury is the administrative centre of a fast developing county, itself threatening to become a satellite of metropolis with 632,487 inhaibants (1993).

Between the retreat of wild animals, where man rarely if ever trod, and the modern, industrial and commuter town, lies the story of a community of predominantly farming folk who prospered, secured a charter and shortly after abandoned its privileges, built and lost a castle, suffered grievously in the Civil War, yet survived, was party to some of the most corrupt electoral manipulations of British politics, yet supported Wilkes as the champion of individual liberty, and was finally overtaken by the accident of lying on the main route out of London to the rich Midlands.

Aylesbury is a town of some 60,000 souls, yet it is a town that some say has lost its own soul. In 1974 it did lose its separate powers, as part, perhaps appropriately, of the then new Aylesbury Vale District.

Gone is the market which gave it purpose and attracted the power-seekers who follow wealth; gone are the old traders, the craftsmen, the horse dealers, sheep drovers, cattlemen, and in their place have risen modern factories on modern estates, modern shops, modern homes, a modern market, and a modern castle housing county administration, moated by the ring road.

Wilkes, who served the town and county and some say exploited both, would be pleased to see his principles at free play in this new place.

Yet there is character left in side streets and squares, and a purposeful air about the people who live and work and trade here. Today the new Aylesbury that the planners coveted has after all risen from the rubble of the old town, burnt at the stake of twentieth century progress.

The swan of Bucks still guards the old Borough arms of Aylesbury—a royal bird for a civil town. This book sets out to tell the story of the town, to record the significant and the curious about its past, and in some small measure to reflect the spirit of individual achievement that typifies the people. In no sense a detailed chronicle, it represents a personal view of this capital town of Buckinghamshire.

Bronze Age man was here — 2,600 years ago in Manor Drive the palstave,
seven socketed axes, two winged axes and other fragments of this 7th/8th
century BC culture were found twenty years ago.
(D. Ottridge County Museum)

The First Ones

When dinosaurs roamed, the Vale was sea. The creatures that died then left their bones behind to wash into the waters, and become today's rare fossil remains. At Hartwell a giant marine pliosaur perished, and another at Watermead. Not far away a meat-eating megolosaurus met his end. At Quainton a long-necked plesiosaurian reptile came to rest, as did his fellow at Westcott, and an icthyosaur joined his larger contemporary at Hartwell. Sharks swam where green fields now lie. Those were the millenia which the experts label the Jurassic and Cretaceous Systems.

In the Pleistocene period around one and a half million years ago, bears had replaced the small-brained reptiles of earlier ages, foraging between Hartwell and Aylesbury; their remains survived at Pitstone. As the Ice Ages came and went so did the mammoth, woolly rhinoceros, bison and spotted hyaena. It may be the splintered bones of a bear were broken open by one of the earliest men to tread our hillsides.

For earliest man was a stranger to Aylesbury. He made occasional forays into the Burnham plateau behind the Chilterns — to Missenden, Chesham and elsewhere — and well to the north, in the Ouse and Ousel valleys, but ten thousand years ago he was still south of these hills, and in the dry valleys of the Chilterns themselves. Then around 5600 BC the so-called Mesolithic or Middle Stone Age men gradually reached us from what we now call Europe, across the land bridge later riven by the Channel.

Those men hunted across the Vale and through the hills. Here was wildwood, where the animals made the tracks, and man followed the line of least resistance, killing for food and clothing. Throughout the area, he scattered fragments of knapped flint, proving his passing but not his permanence. Perhaps he came our way because of the natural gaps in the daunting Chilterns at Risborough and Wendover; perhaps he tarried because here was the precious resource of water in the Tame; perhaps he paused awhile in small family units, because the ground was dry and well drained, on our Portland limestone shelf. His quarry were red deer and the mighty aurochs — wild cattle, six feet at the shoulder.

New Stone Age or Neolithic man, some six thousand years ago, swept in over a period from Europe. These were the first farmers, who certainly settled near Whiteleaf, above the feature known as the Upper Icknield Way and in a fairly tight pattern to its north. There they buried their dead, within sight of later Aylesbury, with their pottery; in the soil of that mound there still survive the impressions of their cereals — our first proof of local cultivation. And in Walton, they settled too — they left behind more than simple flints; their fragments of pottery indicate residence.

Around 1800 BC the dawn of what some call the Bronze Age saw fresh evidence on the ground at Bledlow and the Risboroughs, more left during that millenium; while passing through Aston Clinton, one warrior at least dropped his knife. His fellows left their mark at Walton, and Waddesdon too marks their passage — the sharp celts (tools) of a tradesman found there witness their sojourn. Later still, they spread with some security further afield, and in 8-700 BC they may well have secured a home at Aylesbury itself, leaving axes and other fragments of their culture near the Tindal hospital — perhaps the first men to truly till Aylesbury soil. One of their womenfolk was buried, her remains placed in a cremation urn at Bierton, and someone of that period mislaid his socketed axe right in the centre of later events — on the (old) site of Hampden's statue, in the Market Square.

By the 'Iron Age', three hundred years on, South Bucks was relatively densely peopled, and within 250 years a series of fortified settlements spread along the crown of the Chilterns. Bledlow was a major nearby stronghold. By 100 BC, Bucks was probably ruled by the powerful Belgic tribe, the Catuvellauni. They buried or mislaid coins and other artefacts at Bledlow, Cholesbury, Halton, Kimble, Aston Clinton and Tring. Hard by today's George Street, two skulls, animal bones, pottery sherds, pieces of saddle quern used for grinding corn, a pebble 'pounder' and the post holes of a building have all been rediscovered.

Most exciting of all, near the Prebendal, a ditch some ten feet deep, dating to between the 5th and 6th centuries BC, has been uncovered. This is almost certainly part of an early hill fort complex — an earthwork thrown up to protect a number of people and the earliest indication of an embryo township. There were also contemporary settlements — family units — at Coldharbour Farm and possibly other sites around the future Aylesbury.

The Romans appeared in 55 BC and at subsequent intervals, to suppress the natives and exploit their inter-tribal conflicts. It was they who drove a route, Akeman Street, past Aylesbury. A century before that, a Belgic settlement had developed at Bierton, by the later church site, using imported pottery, exchanging coinage, and building round-houses; a Roman farmstead was planted where Sainsbury's now stands. The Romans drove another track north, towards Towcester, making Fleet Marston something of a crossroads, and a Romano-British staging post, on the direct route to Alcester and the west from their great city of Verulamium (St Albans).

Roman Aylesbury had its heart at Walton Court; here the soldiery stayed — not compliant Romano-Britons, but real Romans — and they left behind military equipment, including a key, harness mount and a spear.

The Romans found Bucks to their liking; their subjects established farms throughout the Chiltern foothills. Romano-British activity spread to Stone, Hartwell, Tythrop, Weston Turville, Bledlow and Bierton, and a Roman pavement bears witness to civilising influences at Little Kimble. Now there were still more, if lesser settlements throughout the region. There may also have been one at Haydon Hill. The Roman habit of establishing farms at two mile intervals, while punctuating the Icknield Way, and certain Chiltern valleys, does not extend to the foothills, where Nash Lee boasts a minor Romano-British structure. Perhaps the inconsistency of the terrain inhibited the usual Roman order.

By now the wildwood was more or less cleared, the land well managed. No longer did man hunt the deer and the aurochs, though doubtless the newly introduced pheasant was a suitable option. Roman Bucks was busy and it was prosperous. These efficient engineers and pastoralists conquered country and countryside; the modern Roman state made Aylesbury a crossroads, exploited and extended the farms it found and set this place on its way as a trading centre.

Once the proud Romans relinquished control, some sixteen hundred years ago, the Britons of those unrecorded ages must have finally realised that potential, making a sustained effort at permanent, prosperous settlement, for this was soon to become the scene of the bloodiest carnage of the Saxon conquest, and a major Saxon prize.

ABOVE: Over three thousand years back, a Bronze Age warrior dropped this knife dagger at Aston Hill, Halton.

LEFT: A decade before Christ, this Belgic amphora (jar) was in use at Aston Clinton.

RIGHT: In the second century AD a middle class Romanised British lady used this beaker at Weston Turville. (All County Museum)

LEFT: The Roman state held sway over hills and vale—this bottle was buried in a Weston Turville grave, along with BELOW: this European enamelled brooch.

RIGHT: Roman influence extended to Bierton two centuries later where this indented beaker was in use. (All County Museum)

Aiglerburgh

Between the fifth and sixth centuries, of which little is properly known, the Anglo-Saxons colonised growing areas of Britain, and local place-names of apparently Saxon origin include Weedon (weoh—idol) and even possibly Aylesbury itself. Scholars have differed: some say the name derived from the church, but most agree it reflects the town itself: Aigle's Burgh—the homestead of Aigle. So Edlesburie or Aiglerburgh (or any of the 57 varieties of the name ascribed to the place) became part of the Anglo-Saxon kingdom of Mercia (administered by the Angles), and many are the mementoes of their occupation left behind in the Vale, while at Walton itself there were Saxon houses in the fifth century.

The take-over of Aylesbury came about with the sacking of the settlement by West Saxon Cuthwulf — around AD 571. What they won was the hub of a mainly rural region, without proper buildings, domestic ware or coinage — urban life had diminished as the Roman influence waned. Although the Saxons were also farmers, they were a sometimes violent race — the Saxon buried at Bledlow had both his arms broken during his lifetime.

Dates for those times are somewhat suspect, but the record says that in AD 429 the Saxons had been less successful. It is possible that St Germanus and his Britons beat the Saxons and Picts in the Chilterns battle said to take place that year — but the evidence is slim. The Saxon victory of 571 was one of a series of four which set the seal on Saxon settlement in the region, growing since about AD 500. They established a major burial ground at Cursley Hill, two miles SW from the town — between Hartwell and Bishopstone — in which have been found articles of Roman design, probably hangovers from Romanised British families. It may well be that the Saxons had been merging peaceably with the indigenous population all along the Chiltern chain of settlements, long before the sixth century conquest; the Romans had certainly imported Germanic mercenaries with their legions, many of whom would have remained and blended with their British contemporaries.

Hartwell became a Saxon place — there they left their weapons. At Stone they buried their dead, and with one of them a fine brooch. Bishopstone has yielded another. At Eythrop warriors left equipment but Dinton is so far the richest of Saxon sources. Here the cemetery embraced twenty burials of the late 5th - early 6th centuries and into the shades of darkness they took with them grave goods to make life after death that much richer — brooches, beads, a bucket and a spear. Walton was occupied by Saxons in the fifth century.

By the seventh or eighth century the Cilternsaetan tribe had established itself firmly in the Vale, taking its name from the hills behind; Aylesbury was now a crossroads, a focus for the region and Christianity had begun to catch the imagination and souls of its people.

Aylesbury's church was raised by the Saxons — legend gives it as St Osyth's burial place, but that is not proven. What is certain is the specific evidence in the Prebendal ditch — eighth century substantive traces, probably contemporary with the founding of Aylesbury's minster church, plus other excavated burials which strongly suggest a Middle Saxon building where St Mary's now stands — there was certainly a late Saxon church in the town.

It is becoming gradually clearer that Saxon Aylesbury was a fortified burgh. Examination of building works at the junction of Temple and Bourbon Streets two decades ago yielded traces of a possible late Saxon ditch, which fell into disuse by the twelfth century. Some fragments of pottery suggested a Saxon presence. There is a conjectural alignment with the Prebendal ditch. That ditch, probably part of the burgh's defence, could well be the basis for a later earthwork — Aylesbury's missing 'castle'. Such a raised rampart may have been used from time to time as part of the defences surrounding a fortified place. There is no doubt the Saxons dug this ditch; so perhaps they were also responsible for the most believed, unproven monument the town can claim.

Certainly the Danes were much feared invaders, who ravaged the Vale in AD 921, taking wholesale spoil in captives and cattle between Bernwood and Aylesbury. Some Danish weapons were wrested from their owners' hands or dropped in these skirmishes that raged not far from the town, and an axe of uncertain origin suggests conflicts at Holman's Bridge, where it was found in 1855, together with a Saxon spear. The Danes put their hallmark on Tythrop, Eythrope, Bixthorpe—all Danish derived place-names.

The later Saxon occupation crystallised with the Lady of Aylesbury, Edith, Christian daughter of Panda of Mercia, who was succeeded by Alefheah, who in turn died in 971 AD and bequeathed the town to King Eadgar, when Aylesbury became an administrative centre for the first time. By the eleventh century, the Saxons were once again undisputed masters of the kingdom. The mint was already established under Ethelred I, and maintained by Cnut the Dane. In 1042 Edward the Confessor mounted the throne, striking coinage at a town he must have regarded as one of the jewels in his crown—Aylesbury.

The Saxons buried their dead at Bishopstone, along with two fine shoulder brooches, *c* 500AD. (County Museum)

ABOVE : This 6th century AD Saxon spearhead
was left behind at Bishopstone.

LEFT: The later Saxons dug this ditch around the 'town' of Aylesbury.

CENTRE : Bicester Road, near Quarrendon yielded this Saxon
scramasaxe or sword knife.

RIGHT : Saxon soldiery passed over Holmans Bridge—and one
left his spear behind thirteen centuries ago. (All County Museum)

LEFT: A vicious spear from a Viking warrior, plundering Aylesbury Vale in the 10th century AD.

ABOVE: Edward the Confessor made money in the town: his silver penny (obverse). (Both County Museum)

BELOW: Edward instructs Harold in the 11th century—from the Bayeux tapestry. (Mansell Collection)

ABOVE: The reverse of the silver penny minted here. (County Museum)

LEFT: A Dane dropped this spear at Aylesbury. (County Museum)

RIGHT: The ancient Hundreds of Buckinghamshire.

ÍERRA REGIS.

[Latin Domesday manuscript text reproduced as a facsimile image]

ABOVE: The King's land: Aylesbury's entry in the Domesday survey of 1086.
(By permission of HM Controller of the Stationery Office)

BELOW: The key of a 12th century door at Aylesbury. (County Museum)

Land of Kings

Edward the Confessor benefited from his Aylesbury holdings to the tune of £25 annually, whereas Buckingham was worth only £10. By the time William I had accepted the crown at Berkhamsted Castle in 1066, there were three separate hundreds which later became part of Aylesbury Hundred — Elesberie, Risberge and Stanes (Aylesbury, Risborough and Stone). Elesberie itself included the town with Walton, Aston Clinton, Bierton, Buckland, Broughton, Ellesborough and Stoke Mandeville.

At the time of the Domesday Survey in 1086, Aylesbury produced at least £10 in tolls alone, being the centre of a number of important roads. Yet little trade centred on the town.

Aylesbury, or Eilseberia, as the Normans called it, was King's land, assessed at 16 hides (120 acres in economic, not territorial terms); it supported 16 plough teams, and two on the home farm. Twenty villeins (tied tenants) together with fourteen bordars (menial cottagers) worked ten ploughs, but could have been increased to fourteen in the opinion of the surveyors. There were two serfs (even lower than bordars in the feudal pecking order), and two mills worth 23 shillings. There was sufficient grazing to support eighty oxen, and the manor was upgraded to yield £56 to the King plus the £10 tolls. There was also one sokeman (free tenant) who held about 30 acres which he could dispose of at will, while serving the King's sheriff.

The town remained in the Crown's direct possession until 1204 when King John granted it to Geoffrey Fitz Piers, Earl of Essex for £60 pa. Sixty-two years later, another Earl of Essex saw fit to side with Simon de Montfort, and lost the manor back to the Crown. Gilbert, Earl of Clare became lord, but two years later Aylesbury was once again Essex land. Descending through the female side of the family, the manor eventually came into the hands of James Butler, Earl of Ormonde—in 1332; he settled it on his wife Eleanor, granddaughter of Edward I, and when he died four years later, she inherited. The rents were by then worth £225 annually. Her son passed it on to his boy, whose wife let it in his absence in Ireland, unfortunately to tenants who became involved in the 1400 plot to overthrow Henry IV. The estate was once again seized by the Crown.

The Ormondes regained the estate five years later, but in 1461 the Ormonde son and heir, James, Earl of Wiltshire, now in possession, found himself on the wrong (Lancastrian) side of the Crown, and was attainted. Yet again Aylesbury was back under Crown rule, and Edward IV granted it to Henry, Earl of Essex. It took 24 years for James to regain royal favour, and the estate was returned to his younger brother Thomas—seventh Earl of Ormonde.

Ormonde's daughter married Sir William Boleyn, and she and her son Thomas, who was Earl of Ormonde and Wiltshire, parted with Aylesbury to Sir John Baldwin—the man who presided over the trial of Anne Boleyn—the 'Fair Maid of Aylesbury'. Baldwin died in 1545, and left Aylesbury to his two grandsons, Sir Thomas Pakington from Worcestershire, and John Borlase. The two resolved the title in favour of Pakington in 1551, who also successfully resisted a Boleyn takeover bid, and the Pakingtons held Aylesbury for 91 years, when their Royalist sympathies cost them the estate until the Restoration. Pakingtons dominated the manor and to a degree the town, thenceforth. Over two centuries later, the last direct male descendant, Sir John sold out to George, Marquess of Buckingham—in 1802. In 1848 Acton Tindal, clerk of the peace for the county, bought it for £5,000, and in 1884 he sold up to John Parker. Today the manorial rights and obligations are virtually non-existent.

While Aylesbury was a town with a lord, and not strictly speaking a straightforward manor, there were other estates around the town. One such was Otters Fee, or Otterers Fee, originally granted by Henry II to Roger Follus, his otter hunter, in 1179, in return for straw for the Royal bed and two geese and three eels should the Royal presence be felt in the town. The manor passed down through the family, who styled themselves Fitz Richard, until the Baldwins came into possession halfway through the 15th century, and the manor was joined with Aylesbury proper. The land was situated between Temple Square and Rickfords Hill.

Castle Fee was located in the Castle Street area, and comprised lands probably granted originally to a personal soldier or servant of an 11th century king, and this manor also came to the Baldwins in the early 16th century.

The delightfully named Bawd's Fee, probably sited between the Crown and Kings Head behind the original Market Square, also came into the ubiquitous Baldwin hands at the turn of the 16th century, passed to the Pakingtons, and disappeared from the records within a hundred years.

The Manor of Walton was for the most part in the hands of the Church. It formed part of the revenue of a Lincoln Cathedral holding, and was mentioned in William II's charter to the cathedral. It was variously leased to laymen until 1650 when a linendraper called William Meade, bought it and sold it three years later. The cathedral regained the manor subsequently, and in 1840 it passed into the hands of the Ecclesiastical Commissioners.

The so called Prebendal Manor of Aylesbury, or Parsonage Manor, was another church estate—and had been so as far back as 1053 when it belonged to the see of Dorchester. William I transferred the estate to Lincoln, and William II confirmed the arrangements. The estate included land in Walton, Stoke Mandeville and Buckland. The church and manor tended to operate in tandem, and the dean enjoyed the benefits and presumably discharged the obligations of the manor. However, in 1250 or so, he lost them, and in 1290 after some diocesan changes moving the manorial incomes around, the King siezed the manor, and gave it to a notorious collector of church livings, Robert de Baldock. This annoyed both Bishop and Pope.

During the 16th century the manor appears to have come under the leasehold control of the Pakingtons, and later the Lees. Other lessees included Madam Meade, whose daughter Mary married John Wilkes—which is how he came to be so indelibly associated with the house that bears the manorial name. In 1864 the Ecclesiastical Commissioners sold the material aspects of the manor—incomes, house and land.

There were other landlords in Aylesbury. The Verney family of North Bucks held lands at Fleet Marston and Middle Claydon, and in 1465 other lands at Aylesbury, Burcote and Bierton which passed to the Verneys from William Wandesford, courtesy the Crown. These estates included the ancient tavern, the Kings Head, whose great hall had probably just been built at that time. It may be that Essex left some control of Aylesbury in Verney hands during this period.

Ralph Verney was Steward of the manor, and in 1465 became Lord Mayor of London; the family fortunes were well and truly laid. John Ingram held the manorial courts in Verney's absence, held the lease of the Prebendal Manor, and collected the tithes.

John Balky was Master of the Gild of St Mary which was founded in 1450 basically as a welfare organisation stemming from church interests, but which took an active, and sometimes effective interest in town affairs. He was also Bailiff for Essex's lordship 1461-1486. He kept accounts, rode to London three times a year with the fee farm of the town and took the books to Coventry for auditing.

Balky was responsible for letting the manorial home farm at Walton, where the principal crop was rushing for thatch. The manor house was Walton Court, and it was Balky's job to protect it against marauders. He kept it stockaded and moated, and kept the timber-framed wattle and daub walls in good repair. (Bricks were then a novelty.) He put Richard Sharpe, reeve, in charge of the farm itself, and Sharpe had two permanent, resident workers —James and Thomas. The rest of the labour force held their own tenancies as well. Fifty acres were down to hay and meadows were rented from other farms, such as Honyam Moor and Warner Hook.

Essex had the right to keep livestock and goods abandoned by their owners; he may also have exercised another manorial right—to have a counterfeiter hanged, drawn and quartered!

The manorial responsibilities were wide and varied. Spittle Mill belonged to the estate at one time; the lord was expected to keep the Moot Hall in the market place in good repair; the Bull's Head was his hospice which he extensively repaired in 1447/8 and again five years later. At mid-century some idea of the manorial establishment can be gauged from his transport fleet—65 horses and hackneys, a squire and 15 grooms in charge. His annual repair bill for a year was £7 11s 3d.

The lords of Aylesbury appear not to have had a particularly easy ride. The townspeople were granted certain rights and from time to time there was friction. In the 12th century there is early evidence of such rights, and in the 14th century town and lord were certainly at loggerheads, mostly over the right to commonland for grazing.

The townspeople charged tolls for crossing Walton Bridge—and kept it in repair, in the 14th century, and the 15th saw the rise of the Gild. In the last year of that century the townsmen were complaining again—about the lord's failures to organise the court records properly, to provide a moot hall, pillory and cucking-stool. In the next two centuries they fought constantly for further privileges, especially when it came to common land facilities, and they gained their first charter in 1554. The charter was a direct challenge to lord of the manor Pakington. He was, after all, hereditary lord of the entire town, except the church manor, which he leased anyway. He held the purse strings, the legal power, and the commercial privileges. He also enjoyed most of the resultant incomes. Now the town was slipping from his grasp. His power was enormous, and the townsmen appear to have been sufficiently overawed not to dare to implement their hardwon borough rights. He took umbrage, enclosed the common lands and his widow, Dorothy took it upon herself to elect the town's member of parliament!

The Civil War temporarily broke the lord's stranglehold, but on the Restoration, the Pakingtons came back with a vengeance, and with Royal support, regained most of their former rights and privileges, except that of producing the town's MP. 1771 enclosures of commons, and the transfer of the market to private enterprise and finally local government, eventually resolved the dissensions of centuries.

Aylesbury's actual Manor House, built in the 13th century, survived until the 16th century, was probably in Kingsbury, on the site of the Victorian building, later destroyed too. The seat of later lords was in Walton, and the Pakingtons themselves lived in the Friary — destroyed in the Civil War. Now there is nothing left of manor or house — save the Kings Head itself.

ABOVE: The grant by John, son of Geoffrey FitzPeter to Hugh the cook, of a virgate in Aylesbury and a meadow between Froxefeld Bridge and the maladarium (hospital) outside the town; c1250.
(Bucks Archaeological Society)

LEFT BELOW: 14th century religion: a cross from Friars Croft.
(County Museum)

RIGHT BELOW: The arms of Robert Lee, later knight of Quarrendon.

ABOVE: Rental and notebook of the bailiff of the Manor of Aylesbury.
(Worcestershire Record Office)

Parson's Fee. (Hayward Parrott)

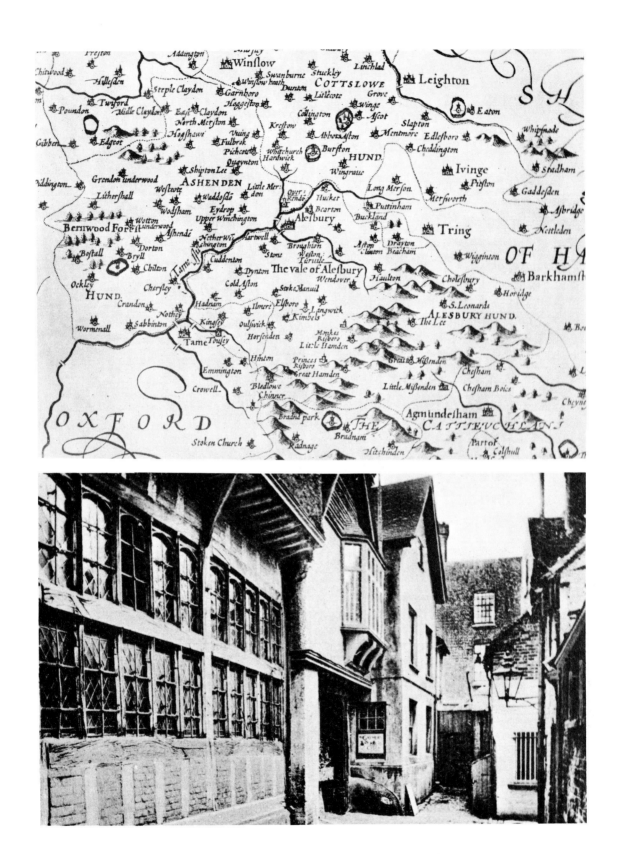

ABOVE: The Aylesbury area in 1610. (Osterfield collection)

BELOW: The Old King's Head. (Ralph May)

28

ABOVE: John Pakington signed this 16th century document conveying property in the Manor of Aylesbury and Abbotts-Broughton to settle his debts. (Bucks Archaeological Society)

LEFT BELOW: The Brudenels were styled Earls of Aylesbury, the d'Ailesbury family perhaps holding local lands in the 12th century

RIGHT BELOW: The Grenvilles (Temples) dominated county affairs and influenced town matters. (Both Margaret Sale)

ABOVE: The boundaries of the Manor of the Rectory of Aylesbury are detailed in this Court Roll of May 20, 1791, signed by Steward John Parker. (Bucks Archaeological Society)

LEFT BELOW: Prebendal House. (Osterfield)

RIGHT BELOW: Sir John Pakington, Baron Hampton, who sold the Manor of Aylesbury to the Marquess of Buckingham in 1802. (Mansell Collection)

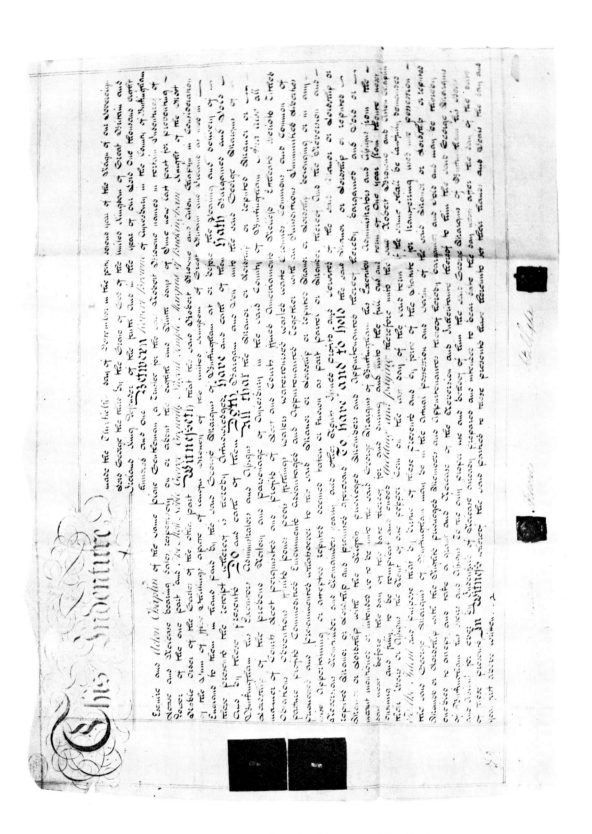

George Grenville Nugent Temple, Marquess of Buckingham, acquired
the Prebendal Manor in 1801 by this indenture. (County Record Office)

The Particulars and Conditions of Sale
OF THE VERY VALUABLE
FREEHOLD MANOR
OF
Aylesbury with Bierton,
WITH QUIT RENTS AMOUNTING TO £33. 9s. 2d. PER ANNUM, FINES, &c.

The MANOR of the RECTORY of AYLESBURY,
With the RIGHT OF APPOINTING CONSTABLES; also,
THE MANOR OF BROUGHTON STAVELY,
With QUIT RENTS amounting to £8. 5s. 7d. per Annum, FINES, &c.

THE TOLLS OF THE AYLESBURY MARKET, &c.
Let at EIGHTY-FIVE POUNDS per Annum.

The MANOR HOUSE, Garden & Land,
Extending from KINGSBURY to the High Road to BUCKINGHAM,
AND
FOUR DWELLING HOUSES ADJOINING.

THE BULL CLOSE,
A Valuable Piece of PASTURE LAND, eligible for BUILDING UPON,
AND ABUTTING ON THE TURNPIKE ROAD.
With Extensive Yard and Farming Buildings, in White Hill Street,
And FIVE COTTAGES NEAR THE CHURCHYARD.

ALSO

THE REVERSION after the death of Mr. BARTON, aged 64 Years,

TO A

Freehold House & Butcher's Shop, Slaughter House, &c.
IN THE BUCKINGHAM ROAD.

Which will be Sold by Auction,
BY MESSRS

FAREBROTHER, CLARK and LYE

AT THE GEORGE INN, AYLESBURY,
On FRIDAY, the 5th day of MAY, 1848,
AT TEN FOR ELEVEN O'CLOCK PRECISELY.—IN LOTS.

Particulars may be had of Messrs TINDAL and SON, Solicitors, Aylesbury; at the Place of Sale; Red Lion, Wendover; Cobham Arms, Buckingham; Angel, Oxford; Bell, Winslow; of Messrs. LIGHTFOOT, ROBSON and LIGHTFOOT, Solicitors, Castle Street, Leicester Square; at Garraways; and at Messrs. FAREBROTHER, CLARK and LYE's Offices, 6, Lancaster Place, Strand.

Printed by J. DAVY and SONS, 137, Long Acre.

Aylesbury's Manors were up for sale in 1848.
(Bucks Reference Library)

32

BUCKINGHAMSHIRE.

Particulars and Conditions of Sale
OF A

VALUABLE FREEHOLD AND TITHE FREE

PROPERTY,
AT

AYLESBURY & PRINCES RISBOROUGH;

Comprising at AYLESBURY,

THE PREBENDAL HOUSE,

A CAPITAL FAMILY MANSION,

In perfect Repair, with excellent Offices, Stabling, Coach-house, &c., and every convenience for a Family of the highest respectability; and large Gardens and Paddock, containing altogether upwards of Four Acres.

ALSO,

SEVERAL CLOSES OF RICH PASTURE LAND,

Lying adjoining the Town of Aylesbury, and a

A LARGE PIECE OF GROUND adjoining the Turnpike Road to Tring,

Lately used as a NURSERY GARDEN, admirably adapted for BUILDING PURPOSES,

ALSO,

A GROUND RENT OF £20 per Annum,

With the Reversion in Fee of the newly-erected Dwelling Houses and Premises on which the Rent is secured.

ALSO,

TWO COTTAGES, in the CHURCH-YARD.

And at PRINCES RISBOROUGH,

The Valuable Manors of Princes Risborough and Abbots Risborough,

With extensive Woodlands, containing, together with some Cottages, Gardens, and Closes of Land, 280 Acres, or thereabouts.

ALSO,

AN EXCELLENT PIECE OF ARABLE LAND, at Longwick,

Known as "NORTH FIELD," containing nearly 17 Acres,

Which will be Sold by Auction by

Mr. J. GADSDEN,

AT THE GEORGE HOTEL, AYLESBURY,

ON WEDNESDAY, the 14th of MAY, 1851,

At One for Two o'Clock precisely, in Lots,

(By Order of the Trustees under the Will of the late Thomas Tindal, Esq.)

Particulars and Conditions of Sale may be had of Messrs. TINDAL & BAYNES, Solicitors, Aylesbury; and of Messrs. WOODROOFFE, Solicitors, No. 1, New Square, Lincoln's Inn; at the principal Inns in Aylesbury and Princes Risborough; of Mr. HUMPHREY BULL, Land and Estate Agent, Aylesbury; and of the Auctioneer, Aylesbury.

☞ *The Lots may be Viewed with the permission of the respective Tenants, and the Woods on application to Thomas Parslow, the Woodman.*

The executors of Thomas Tindal sold up the Prebendal House in 1851.
(County Record Office)

33

ABOVE: The Manor House, built in 1852 and demolished two years ago.
(Hayward Parrott)

BELOW: The end of the Manor House. (E. D. Hollowday)

Monks and Martyrs

There was a Saxon church at Aylesbury by the 9th century. There was probably one earlier than that. But whether the church stood on its present site or not is not yet proven. Legend and fact have become confused, and the alleged holy waters at Quarrendon, where some say St Osyth was beheaded by the Danes may well have been at Bierton — if indeed they existed at all. St Edburg and St Edith were born at Quarrendon, and St Osyth was reputedly their niece. St Edith is said to have founded a nunnery at Aylesbury. The trouble is that St Osyth is also claimed to have acquired her martyrdom in Essex. The truth possibly lies with two St Osyths, though the saint's remains were venerated up to 1500, when the local shrine was dismantled by papal decree.

Whatever the truth of the legends, Aylesbury was from Saxon times the ecclesiastical centre of Bucks—receiving payments in grain from no less than eight surrounding hundreds. William I took the church from the see of Dorchester and transferred it to Lincoln diocese. It was worth having: Aylesbury yielded £20 a year to the Bishop's coffers, whereas Buckingham produced a miserable 30s. There were four dependent chapels until 1294 (Bierton, Quarrendon, Stoke Mandeville and Buckland) and in 1280 a synod (national church meeting) was held in the town. In 1291 Aylesbury was valued at £133 6s 8d along with the two other livings it incorporated.

The church, including some Norman elements, was built in the first half of the 13th century, and on the highest site in the town. It was extended in the 15th century and suffered grievously in the Civil War. In 1642 one of Cromwell's men, Nehemiah Wharton wrote that the vicar Penruddock, 'a Papist' was set upon and his church windows defaced, and the 'holy railles' burnt. After the War the church moved out of the Bishop's patronage, and no post-war records survive. The Prebendal house was in the hands of Wilkes by 1767 when the vestry determined to erect a gallery in the church, and he sat on the relevant committee. In 1765, a surveyor, Mr Keen reported on the poor state of the building; he opined that it might stand until he got to Watford. There was little local reaction. In 1781 the gallery project came up again, and a faculty was obtained to build it. But by the 19th century, part of the church was used as a fire depot, and before that it had done duty as a gunpowder store. In 1848 the bell fastenings gave way, the congregation panicked, and Gilbert Scott was called in.

Meanwhile other matters had engaged local men. As far back as 1494 John Stone had left by will certain rent incomes to provide a clock and chimes, and in 1691 John Aylward followed suit; in 1854 a new clock was eventually erected for £451. The clock that preceded it was inscribed:

I labour here with all my might,
To tell the hour both day and night;
Then you a lesson take by me,
And serve your God as I serve thee.

The bells were also inscribed, the smallest thus:

I men to make it understood,
That though I'm little, yet I'm good.

These were dated 1773 and made by Peck and Chapman of London; they replaced the 1733 bells. The saint's bell dated back to 1612. Music was much in mind, and in 1782 Mary Pitches gave an organ to the church; this was much improved in 1853 and fully restored two years later.

Religious legend abounds in Aylesbury: there was Radulphus Ruebairn, an extraordinary monkish gentleman who shut himself in his cell to read holy writ, was assumed to have died, and amazed his brothers when he surfaced days later, apparently none the worse for his fast.

Then again, Ulfric the anchorite moved to Aylesbury in 1190—he was another faster, and something of a miracle worker. He saved a man possessed during his lifetime, and accomplished sundry other marvels—posthumously!

Walter de Whyteforde completes a trilogy of legendary characters: in 1240 he conceived a love for a lady about to take holy vows. He tried every trick to obtain her favours, failed, was struck by disease, vowed to God he would repent, recovered, and dedicated and built a monastery at Aylesbury—or so it is said.

In fact a friary was founded in Aylesbury, in 1386, but by James Botelier, third Earl of Ormonde, then lord of the town. It was a Franciscan or Grey Friars' establishment and lasted until the dissolution in 1536. Commissioner Dr John London found little to criticise in the way of wealthy accoutrements among the friars: they were poor, and their ornaments 'coarse'. He defaced the church but left the home unscathed. There were at one time more than sixty monks in residence, but London found only six or seven.

Certainly the friary was important — the local lords had always been buried there. Now the church was destroyed, and the friary was surrendered by a deed of October 1. Although poor, its buildings were not. The Baldwins acquired it and made it their country seat and later the Pakingtons occupied it. Then Cromwell's men finally destroyed it. It is believed to have been at the foot of Rickford's Hill.

Aylesbury's churchmen were not unmindful of the needs of others. The Trinitarians founded a leper hospital, at the Hartwell end of the town in the 14th century — hence the corruption of one local place name: Spittle Mill. This was originally the Hospital of St Leonard.

A formally religious foundation, the chantry, or Gild or St Mary was founded in 1450 by local men in concert with Chancellor Cardinal Kemp and the Archbishop of York. It soon took an active interest in town affairs, and found itself confronting the lords of the manor on more than one occasion. The gild was suppressed in 1547 along with the friary. Its Brother House was near the churchyard.

The churchyard itself, in common with other towns, was a medieaval centre of entertainment, for Mother Church provided learning and leisure facilities, as well as a sound mind and spirit. Religious plays were performed there in the 16th century, but the following century there were questions asked as to the proprieties of churchyard activities. It was by then the site of sports, games, cockfights and elections, and ruffians gathered there for nefarious purposes. By the 19th century the south side was reserved for Christian burial and the north for unconsecrated ones. It was the local school playground, and footpaths criss-crossed it. Parsons Fee was once part of the whole, since diminished. In 1857 Tring road cemetery was opened.

Meanwhile in 1848 Scott had delivered his report, and a damning one it was. He referred to 'the universal failure of the foundation of the original' building and went on to say there was 'scarcely one wall or pillar of the original date, which had not gone out of the perpendicular', and 'the pillars of the Nave lean westward to a frightful extent.' The church was said to be founded on rock. Not so, said Scott. It was based on loose earth and stones, much buttressed and piered with inferior materials. The succession of failures went back a long way, with sorry efforts to sort them out. Scott said the bodies buried near the church would have to be exhumed and removed, concrete poured into the foundations, and iron ties put to the tower. The stonework would have to be replaced piece by piece to save the latter, and new timbers inserted. In 1855 the initial restoration was implemented and by 1869 the final touches completed. In 1870 new stained glass windows were installed. In all £16,000 was spent.

Not long after Scott's report, Bishop Wilberforce of Oxford was to preach at St Mary's, and he did not want the force of his sermon lost when the church clock struck. He asked the verger to handle the problem, and the clapper was secured to a pew. Came the hour, the clock struck, the clapper strained, the pew mountings gave way, up went the pew, the clock made a frightful din, and the audience was more than distracted—it was frightened out of its wits and fled, fearing the dissolution of the entire structure.

If the fabric of the church was much changed and renewed in the last century, a much earlier vestment cupboard survived, with swinging brackets for cassocks and surplices. Scott was not the first to insist on proper repairs. Earlier the same century in 1842 the absentee prebend was forced by local pressure to repair the chancel for £300—replacing 'lead for lead, oak for oak and stone for stone.'

Such was not the fortune of Quarrendon chapel, despite the noble connections of legendary St Osyth. Long deserted and desolate, it was reported in the 19th century as 'eroded' for spare timber, stone and even windows taken for someone else's ornamental summer house, while marble embellishments were hacked out to provide a local craftsman with a living—turning out candle sticks.

Thieves took 2 cwt of lead in 1824, recovered by the constables — but no one owned the chapel, so the thieves got away scot free.

While the fabric of St Mary's was a recurring problem, resolved *pro tem*, the spiritual fabric of the church was also questioned: in 1622 on July 28 a visitation by the Bishop found that 22 people had failed to attend divine service, and that Richard Dalby had taught school without a licence. John Tilbie, who had married his dead brother's wife, and been excommunicated, petitioned for revocation.

In 1773 the vestry agreed that 'no allowance should be made for killing sparrows or vermin' in the churchwardens' accounts, and in 1779 they decided 'that no hog, sow, pig be suffered to go about the churchyard.' Any found would be impounded and a fine of a shilling for each animal levied. The eighteenth century threw up some other incidents: in 1701 two one-legged people wed, and in 1737 John Holloway married Susan Childe—his fifth wife.

But more serious exceptions had emerged in the 15th century. In 1464 the market place was the scene of a mass penance by heretics from other Bucks towns. Two centuries later Quakers were in trouble for refusing to pay tithes—three years' prison resulted. Thomas Ellwood was arrested in 1655 and imprisoned in 1656. Isaac Penington found himself in Aylesbury Gaol six times between 1660 and 1670, and was once removed to a malthouse behind the gaol 'not fit for a doghouse'. Dissidents were put there because the gaoler knew their principles prevented any escape attempts. Penruddock was ejected from his living on the other hand, for Papist leanings. He came back at the Restoration. The early 18th century saw considerable backsliding in religious observance at St Mary's—only seven communions were held in 18 years.

Meanwhile in the 17th century, nonconformists were meeting in Benjamin Keach's house at Winslow. In 1678 local farmer's son Monk saved the lives of twelve condemned Aylesbury heretics, including his father and a minister, Stephen Dagnall, by direct intercession with King Charles II. In 1707 the Presbyterian Hale Leys Chapel was formed. Bakers Lane provided a site for the Baptists' meeting place in 1733, while the Quakers were meeting in Rickford's Hill in 1784 and the Independents moved in 1834 from their original 1788 Castle street premises to the Hale Leys chapel, rebuilt in 1874. In 1828 the Walton Street Strict Baptist Chapel was built; in 1837 the Wesleyan chapel was erected. The Primitive Methodists settled in at Station Street in 1845, moving in 1883 to Dell's Mount Place while the Open Brethren met at the Corn Exchange, and by 1878 in the Assembly Rooms. They moved to the north-east corner of the churchyard at St Mary's two years later.

St John's Church was built in 1883, Walton Church in 1845; the Catholic St Joseph's was first established as a mission in 1888 and a temporary iron church erected in 1892, demolished in 1935 and rebuilt by 1937. The Congregational Church went up in 1874 and the Methodist Church in 1894. The Primitive Methodists used the 1882 church until 1951, thereafter joining the Methodist Church, and the Strict Baptist Church was rebuilt in 1895. The General Baptists Southcourt Church was opened in 1930. From 1841 the Friends' Meeting House was unused until it was reopened in 1933, and the Salvation Army Hall was opened in 1928.

Church and charity go hand in hand, and Aylesbury was not without its good intentions. There were at one time over twenty charitable foundations in the town.

In 1493 John Bedford left £600 worth of property to maintain the roads and provide alms for the poor. In 1675 Thomas Hickman left homes and incomes from lands for the poor: Hickman's almshouses.

William Harding in 1719 left property to provide clothing for the poor and pay for apprenticeships for poor children. Unhappily the almshouses erected as a result of Thomas Elliott's gift of 1494 were destroyed by fire, but some incomes continued to the relief of the poor.

In 1567 Robert Brickett left £2; in 1604 William Findall gave £6 13s 4d for poor, prisoners, and a church cleaner; in 1623 William Swaddon gave £3 12s for the poor; in 1735 Mary Syms left monies for poor, retired tradesmen.

Widows benefited from Elizabeth Eman's will of 1723, and Mary Cockman left property incomes to the vicar and the needy—but her charity died 99 years after she did. William

Cockman's almshouses were sold to help pay for the workhouse some three centuries after his gift, and Sir Richard Lee's 1611 gift of rents for the relief of two widows was lost completely by 1885. In 1829 Stephen Holloway left £2,000 to the town's poor.

Perhaps Jacob Clements was in a way the most charitable, for he started working life in Aylesbury as a lace maker. He tired of that, became a pot boy at the Kings Head, then left for London, joining a stockbroker as an office junior, and eventually amassing £300,000. Of this he invested sufficient to provide an annual sum of £40 for the poor of his old town.

In 1974 Scott was entirely vindicated for an original assessment of £15,000 for repairs to St Mary's was totally inadequate. The Church Council, County Council and others decided on a major restoration — and a courageous policy to return the church to its historic role as the centre of the community.

Today St Mary's is in community use five days out of seven. Drama, music (the acoustics are superb), care of mentally and other handicapped children and youth clubs are among its many roles. Altogether £240,000 was found and spent. And William Harding's 1719 charity funded £140,000 of that, the balance publicly subscribed. Some of the money went to replacing pews with chairs, a new organ, choir gallery, kitchen and lavatories. But in 1982 the church ran out of cash. The bells had not been rung for 130 years, because the bellframe was dangerous. The trouble went deeper than estimated, but it was remedied. Happily, Holy Trinity Church, Walton, built in 1845, found the £7,500 it needed in the mid-'70s, when it was reroofed and redecorated. And All Saints, Little Kimble — on the site of the Romano-British settlement at Caena Bella, or Cymbeline — claims the best surviving example of mediaeval wall paintings, over 700 years old, and still in good repair.

ABOVE: St Mary's Parish Church in 1864. (Bucks Reference Library)

ABOVE: This 14th century gilt bronze crucifix once graced the sacristy at
St Mary's. (County Museum)

BELOW: The ancient font of St Mary's, from Lyson's Magna Britannica.

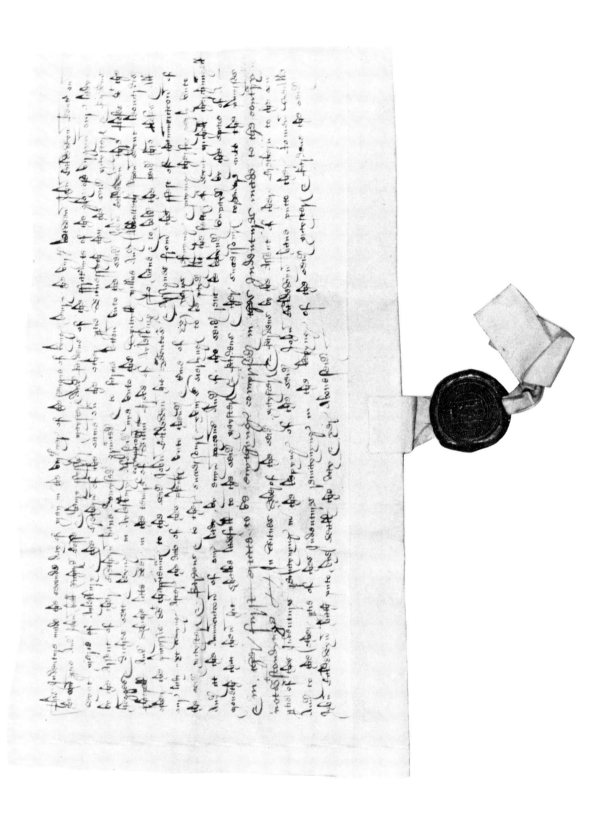

The Masters and Wardens of the Fraternity of the Glorious Virgin Our
Lady St Mary of Aylesbury leased three closes to John Baldwyn on May 2
1517. (Bucks Archaeological Society)

Christeninges

Elzabeth Costerde the daughter of Thomas Coster was baptised the xxiiijth day of Februarij 1564

februarij

Willm Leone the sonne of Thomas Leone was baptized the xxxth of the same moneth

ABOVE: Seal of the Fraternity of the Annunciation on the 1517 deed.
(Bucks Archaeological Society)

BELOW: The first entries in the Parish Register, in 1564.
(County Record Office)

BELOW: The Cemetery in 1864. (Bucks Reference Library)

ABOVE: An 1844 engraving of Aylesbury New Church, consecrated the
following year. (Margaret Sale)

ABOVE: Bedford House, Market Square—left by John Bedford for charitable purposes. (Hayward Parrott)

BELOW: Red Lion Inn, Kingsbury was left by Elizabeth Eman in 1723 to relieve poor widows. (Hayward Parrott)

ABOVE: 'This view is most respectfully inscribed to the Rev John Pretyman, Vicar of Aylesbury, by his obliged old servant, N. Whittock.'

BELOW LEFT: St Martin's Catholic Church—never built. (Both Osterfield)

BELOW RIGHT: Sir George Gilbert Scott. (Mansell Collection)

ABOVE: The Baptist Chapel, Walton Street, built 1828, demolished 1966.
BELOW LEFT: The Old Wesleyan Chapel, Friarage Passage,
demolished 1964/5.

BELOW RIGHT: The old Primitive Methodist Chapel, Buckingham Street,
built 1882. (All Hayward Parrott)

ABOVE: The Methodist Church, Buckingham Street.

RIGHT: The Congregational Church built 1874 in High Street.

BELOW: St John's Church, built 1883 and demolished 1970.
(All Hayward Parrott)

ABOVE LEFT: An Aylesbury divine, the Rev William Gunn.
(Margaret Sale)

ABOVE RIGHT: The Provincial Grand Master opened the Masonic Hall
in 1882. (Hayward Parrott)

BELOW: The rent from this house in Rickford's Hill went to the clock and
chimes charity. (Hayward Parrott)

ABOVE RIGHT: Inside Baker's Lane Chapel. (Osterfield)

ABOVE LEFT: Cllr James Franklin, a 'maker of Methodism' at the turn of the century. (Margaret Sale)

BELOW: Designed for today—St Clare's Catholic Church.

LEFT: This Hanseatic dagger came from Germany, and was used in Aylesbury.

RIGHT: A spur to success on Aylesbury's battlefield? (Both County Museum)

BELOW: John Hampden. (Margaret Sale)

Against the Peace

War has brushed Aylesbury down the centuries. During the Wars of the Roses, the people of the town concentrated on saving lives and property rather than involve themselves with either of the warring factions. It was difficult to know who was on whose side. The Guild of Our Lady was instrumental in the matter. In 1524 the town faced military taxes based on a £37 1s 4d assessment for one of Henry VIII's levies. The Civil War changed Aylesbury's attitude to causes.

Predictably, Charles I's attempt to levy Ship Money in 1635 was not popular. Robert Alexander, bailiff in 1636 collected from Aylesbury Hundred £57 16s 5½d. Two years later three payments had been collected: £11 2s 5d (Stoke Mandeville), £8 17s 11d (Aylesbury) and £5 19s 3d (Stoke Mandeville, Hampden and Wendover). The hundred paid £514 17 9d in 1640. Some paid in kind, with kettles, pots and in one case a colt. By 1642 Richard Grenville noted that Aylesbury Hundreds were taxed £690 6s 9¾d in 1637 and Aylesbury itself paid £43 3s 0d. There were complaints. The tenants of Halton complained en masse through their spokesman Richard Fermor. Defaults there were many, ranging from those who had nothing to give to those who were dead! With this background of protest against Royal demands, it is hardly surprising that Aylesbury was for Parliament in the looming conflict.

The seal was set on Aylesbury's sympathies as the acknowledged centre of the county which sent six thousand petitioners to the House of Commons in 1641 following the great debate on the Grand Remonstrance of 204 objections to the King, and the Royal error in attempting to arrest the five members—including their own John Hampden.

Aylesbury's Members had no difficulty in raising troops in the county; Col Bulstrode commanded the town garrison. Local MP in 1625, Arthur Goodwin, was one of the leaders on the Parliamentary side, and a vocal one at that. He was also John Hampden's friend. But he was succeeded by Sir Edmund Verney of Middle Claydon, and Verney, though a Parliamentarian by conviction, sided with the King through personal loyalty. Sir John Pakington, Lord of the Manor, was a full-time Royalist. No doubt he agreed with the 1685 reporter whose surviving account of the war at Aylesbury referred to this 'horrid rebellion'. By 1640, Sir Ralph Verney, Edmund's son (a Parliamentarian) and Pakington, spoke for Aylesbury in the House. Both were expelled in 1645 and replaced by Thomas Scott and Simon Mayne. Scott was related to the Pakingtons and the Lees and was a pillar of Cromwell's later administration. Mayne came from Dinton Hall. Both were later regicides.

The disposition of forces at the start of the war predictably enough found Buckingham and Aylesbury on opposing sides, with the old enemy staunchly Royalist. Winslow, Bicester, Thame, Brackley, Brill and Haddenham were for the King, and Aylesbury, Hartwell, Wing, Bierton, Waddesdon, Leighton, Wendover, Missenden, Amersham and with some faint interest, Chesham were for Parliament. Aylesburian dissatisfaction harked back to

51

1625 when a letter of discontent was despatched to the hated Villiers, Duke of Buckingham—from the Lord Lieutenant; in 1642 Aylesbury sent a remonstrance to the King, no less, fearful of war and calling for the disbandment of the Royal forces.

The refusal to pay at Great Kimble was one of the first objections nationwide. John Hampden topped the list of those who denied the tax, refusing to pay 31s 6d.

Small wonder that Aylesbury was early selected as a garrison town and military store-house by the government's troops. Lord Wharton commanded initially; a 1642 skirmish with Hampden saw his Royal opponents beaten. Aylesbury was reinforced. Bulstrode became Governor of the town.

On November 1, Holman's Bridge just outside the town saw the first full dress battle at Aylesbury for some thousand years—the so named Battle of Aylesbury. The Royalists under Prince Rupert had some 10,000 of foot and horse, and entered the town Tuesday morning at six. They were not expected, and they gave no warning. The militia foreswore valour for discretion—and entertained them! They also made sure the Prince knew some 6,000 Parliamentarians were en route for the town. In fact Sir William Balfore's force numbered less than 1,500. At Holman's Bridge Rupert charged the soldiery, and the militia jettisoned their good cheer and took him in the rear. Rupert lost. The Parliamentarians suffered 90 dead but took 200 prisoners. The battle raged for a few minutes only, and Rupert retreated to Thame, laying waste as he withdrew. In that same year Sir Edmund Verney lost his hand and his life at Edgehill.

There seemed to be some magnetism to the central Bucks stronghold, for on December 7 Lord Wentworth led a force of 5,000 Royalist troops to the outskirts, thought better of it after viewing the defences, and veered off. Earlier, Rupert's spies had been at work under cover, and reported the militia's state of red alert—one such spy was Sir John Culpeper.

Armed with information, courage, and some thousands of armed men, Rupert marched on the town yet again March 20, 1643, but made no attack. Perhaps Culpeper's report of six field pieces put him off. Earlier it was the town's turn, High Sheriff Grenville taking the militia to battle stations in January, and suffering defeat at Brill Hill. March 13 Rupert retaliated, following up his advantage by attacking Stone with some 6,000 men. But he was foiled in pressing onto Aylesbury by Parliamentarian reinforcements, so he contented himself and no doubt his men by further laying waste. At this time, the garrison was living at the rate of £200 per week. On March 24 Rupert was back, this time with guns—six of them. But to no avail.

Yet soon after, in July, the government's troops were laid low, and driven back into the town. It seemed that Aylesbury was destined for stalemate. Col Aldriche took over the garrison as Governor, and Rupert promptly attempted to suborn him to yield the town. The garrison was now in some distress, and Parliament voted an extra £1,500 for their maintenance. Aldriche would not countenance the King's or his agent's offers.

In January 1644, the King's men were active on two fronts—further cajolery of the town's leaders went hand in glove with bolder efforts—to blow up the town's powder magazine. In May the King's men advanced yet again. Parliament increased the munitions supply. In June 100 Roundheads routed 300 Cavaliers. In June the great man himself visited the loyal town—Cromwell left his sword at Dinton as a memento of the visit. By 1646 matters had quietened down, as far as civil war was concerned, but this had the predictable effect on the garrison locked into a boring billet—they got out of hand, and martial law was declared.

The Civil War saw Aylesbury start and finish as Parliamentarian, with only the traditional leaders—the Lord of the Manor and the Vicar—remaining loyal to the concept of monarchy. One by-product of little benefit to anyone was the £20,000 loss sustained by the Pakington family, who lost their ancient home, though they regained their estates.

War skirted Aylesbury thenceforth. In the late 18th century, during the Napoleonic scares, gentlemen prepared to defend the town against the little Corporal's hordes, and in the 19th century, when the Imperial campaigns were afoot, troops were billeted without request and promptly evicted—troops could not be allowed in an assize town when the assize was in sessions, as a local publican realised, and pointed out.

But it was the Civil War that saw Aylesbury's finest military hour, though one commentator in 1685 saw matters in a different light: '. . . this Towne was . . . filled with Committee-men, Sequestrators, and Purchasers of Church and Crowne lands, who quickly altered the happy constitution of the said place by oppressing and all other ways discouraging the Loyall and dutifull and by Encouraging the Factious and Ribellious.'

The same commentator perhaps put his finger unwittingly on Aylesbury's central truth, that it was a town that survived by combining a sense of right with a sense of fitness. Parliamentarian during the war, it was not slow to accept the Restoration — 'But now that cursed Tribe of villaines are so removed or deade that scarse any ffootstepps of them remayned, and the Towne is much recovered againe for the better.' Less dead perhaps than lying low!

At the close of conflict, the writer estimated that not more than a fifth of the population were dissenters, and 260 out of 300 electors supported a loyal address to the King in 1681. Aylesbury has always understood the winds of change, for in 1696 many signed up with the Association founded to protect King William III following an assassination plot — even though three years earlier Joseph Saxton was one of several who complained against soldiers being billeted on him. In 1696 Thomas Woodward was in difficulties for billeting soldiers in inns throughout the town — except his own.

In 1823 several privates of the 58th Regiment of Foot found Aylesbury less than comfortable when they received fifty lashes in public—for misbehaviour at Buckingham.

Hampden is commemorated by the statue raised to him in 1912, sited in the presumed path of his return from Holman's Bridge in 1642.

The South African War is remembered through the Memorial tablet at the old County Hall, and the statue to Lord Chesham, erected in 1910. Five thousand citizens watched the unveiling in 1921 of the town's War Memorial, commemorating the 264 who lost their lives in World War I and by the addition in 1951 of two tablets, 106 who fell in World War II. Hazell's War Memorial also recalls the sacrifices of 65 employees in the first and 17 in the second wars, and there is a further memorial in the Cemetery to those who lie there from the first war. A Cavalry Memorial was unveiled in the church yard in 1921.

During the last war a land-mine fell near Walton Square in 1940.

In 1956 the town conferred the freedom of the borough on RAF Halton, and in 1967 on the Royal Greenjackets, who had absorbed the Oxford and Bucks Light Infantry.

ABOVE LEFT: Vandyck's portrait of Sir Edmund Verney.

ABOVE RIGHT: Holman's Bridge—site of the Battle of Aylesbury, 1642.
(Hayward Parrott)

BELOW LEFT: Prince Rupert. (Mansell Collection)

BELOW RIGHT: Sir William Balfore. (Mansell Collection)

ABOVE: The volunteers of 1867, Sir Harry Verney in top hat.

LEFT: Capt L. W. Crouch in the full dress uniform of the Bucks Battalion, the Oxfordshire and Bucks Light Infantry.

RIGHT: Col the Viscount Burnham in the full dress uniform of the Bucks Hussars. (All Osterfield)

ABOVE LEFT: Unveiling Lord Chesham's statue. (Bucks Reference Library)

ABOVE RIGHT: Marching as to war. (Margaret Sale)

CENTRE RIGHT: Wounded soldiers, World War I, at Aylesbury.

BELOW LEFT: Local Headquarters of the Oxon and Bucks LI, World War I. (Ralph May)

BELOW RIGHT: Capt Nicholls (bottom row, centre) officer commanding the local soldiery, with his men. (Both Ralph May)

ABOVE: Unveiling the town's War Memorial, in 1921. (Hayward Parrott)

BELOW: World War I tank enters Kingsbury Square as a memorial. Subsequently removed, it blew up—with petrol left in its tank from its last journey. (Ralph May)

A
CALENDAR of PRISONERS,

In Cuſtody in the GAOL at AYLESBURY in the County of BUCKS,

For Felony and Miſdemeanors,

To appear at the next Gaol Delivery to be held at AYLESBURY, for the ſaid County,

On *MONDAY* the Eighth of MARCH, 1784.

RICHARD SCRIMSHIRE, Eſq; Sheriff.

JOHN HORTON,
THOMAS CHOWNDS,
AND
CHARLES COX,
} Remain on their Sentence.

ROBERT MOSS,
EDWARD ARIS,
AND
WILLIAM DAVIS,
} Condemned at Lent Aſſizes, 1783, but afterwards reprieved, remain in Cuſtody.

ISAIAH REDDING,
JAMES ALLEN,
MARY TUSTIN,
GEORGE ROGERS,
WILLIAM HUDSON,
THOMAS LAWRENCE,
ELIZABETH WIGGINTON,
JOHN TUCKER,
AND
JOHN EVANS,
} Sentenced at the laſt Summer Aſſizes to be ſeverally transported for the Term of ſeven Years.

THOMAS WESTFIELD, Committed by Richard Lloyd, Eſq; the 9th of Auguſt, 1783, charged on the Oath of William Barton, of Chepping Wycombe, with feloniouſly ſtealing a brown Mare, the Property of the ſaid William Barton.

18th century offenders. (Bucks Reference Library)

Trying Times

Domesday saw Buckingham as the county town, even if it was worth less than Aylesbury and less accessible. But the combination perhaps of early rights and superior position eventually brought the administration of justice here.

In 1086 when the sheriff distrained cattle, they were impounded in Aylesbury; in 1180 there was a county gaol which served also for the custody of miscreants throughout the King's forest of Bernwood. The townsmen enjoyed the customary rights of tenants of a royal manor, principally separate representation before the justices, and exemption from trial by jury or by battle. Their rights were detailed in a late 12th century charter which recorded the town's 'borough' status, but did not survive—reference is made to it in a later document.

In 1204 the lords of the manor had many privileges, such as their own gallows, tumbrel and pillory, the right to hold estate, hundred and shire courts, and the release from payment of certain taxes usually levied elsewhere.

By 1218 the assizes were established in the town, and in 1276 the town and county gaols were separated. Edward III's charter defined the town's right to its own gaol. It was constantly in a poor state, and escapes were rife. In 1276 the gaoler turned a blind eye to women escapers—at a shilling a head. It was a place worth leaving—smallpox raged, and spread into the town; it was known as 'the gaol fever' and particularly bad outbreaks occurred in 1603, 1665 and 1784. Pigs scavenged there unmolested. In 1682 there was a move for rebuilding. A year later a surveyor was appointed, and a year after that the gaoler, Nathaniel Birtch, petitioned for arrears of rent, claiming eight years at £20 annually. As he was fined £5 at the next sessions for 'suffering the Quakers committed by this Court to goe at lardge' he was probably unsuccessful. He was certainly dismissed.

His successor William Benson did get paid—for small repairs—and in 1692 for looking after 'many dangerous, disorderly and rude prisoners'. In 1693 over £25 was spent on rebuilding two rooms, and one way and another the gaol proved an expense to the county— many mothers died in prison, and as many more gave birth within its none too secure walls. Medical treatment was available, though minimal. John Piddington, apothecary was paid £2 10s for medicines which 'by the blessing of God had good Effect' and Mr Tilcock, 'a chirurgeon', performed an effective miracle—'the cure of one Manne lately Executed for felony.' There were allowances for starving prisoners, and one debtor received 1s 6d from one of his creditors.

There was also a bridewell, or house of correction at Aylesbury, and in 1680 the gallows were rebuilt at a cost of £2 6s. Stocks, cage and pillory existed, though in 1499 townsmen complained there was no place to hold the lord's court, no pillory and no 'cucking stool'.

The 1553 grant of incorporation under Queen Mary's charter included the right to hold a court of record for pleas of debt up to 100s.

In 1699 the stocks were in the news again. Justice of the Peace Francis Ligo said their location 'under a Mudd wall tyled that incloses the garden' of his home was such that 'by the help of the same stocks, persons may with great Ease climb into his garden and rob his house.' The court ordered their removal. They were sited in Buckingham Road as late as 1823 when two men were put in them for being drunk.

The gibbet was first erected in 1773, on July 23, when Edward Corbet was hung in chains for the murder of Farmer Holt. It came down finally in 1860—on August 15.

Meanwhile in the 17th century there had been unsuccessful attempts to move the assizes to Buckingham, but by 1727 the new County Hall was built—allegedly to the design of Sir John Vanbrugh—and a compromise was effected—the summer assize would be at Buckingham, the court otherwise at Aylesbury. Thus the Act of 1748, but one century and one year later, the assize returned to Aylesbury, for good.

In 1685 the lord of the manor was in trouble for not providing a cage and pillory, and again in 1688 for not supplying the town with a ducking stool.

Earlier, in 1682 Henry Monday had been appointed the master of Aylesbury bridewell, a post he lost ten years later. Michael Read was appointed in his place. In 1694 Monday was in difficulties with the court, charged 'concerning his drinking King James his health'— due to local fears of Stuart loyalists. It did not stop his appointment as keeper of the bridewell two years later.

Gaolers were not the only ones to fall from grace. Francis Ligo was in trouble with a fellow JP William Busby when in 1696 he was accused of ignoring accusations of treason. Charles Noy, bodice maker and petty constable complained that treason was charged 'before two justices . . . and no notice taken of it.' Asked to name them, he refused; they brought him to action in the King's Bench for libel.

Another JP acquired some fame. Thomas Wharton, principal Justice in the county kept the records, and also authored 'Lillibullero'—a popular song said to have been instrumental in the downfall of James II. Wharton became an important Whig politician.

William Benson was the gaoler from 1684 to 1700, and constantly requesting payment for repairs and rent. The post was clearly no sinecure. In 1695 he asked for £6 5s for repairs due to damage done by prisoners. Steps were taken to prevent recurrences, and one man was freed six miles away from the town, to prevent any 'revenge he may exercise in the Town for his Confinement.' In 1698/9 thirteen died of the fever, and in 1704 30 suffered from it. The apothecary charged £25 for attendance. In the 1700s there was a great deal of talk about a new gaol, but nothing came of it. The gaoler received a rise—of 100% from 1½d to 3d per prisoner, in 1693, but by 1700 this was down to 2½d—because corn cost less! Bakers were accused of overcharging for the prisoners' bread, which could cost as much as £23 a quarter. William Chandler, who with Mary Pratt was appointed gaol baker in 1700, was dismissed two years later due to complaints by the prisoners that he 'abused them both in the Weight and Bakeing of the County Bread'.

When Henry Munday was appointed bridewell keeper again in 1696 he had to pay £10 to another claimant for the office, and in 1704 he in turn was paid £4 10s for keeping Elizabeth Thomson, 'a poore distracted Vagrant'. In the end Munday was out of pocket, for he had to take on a full-time nurse to look after the sick woman. In 1707 the gaoler had troubles when the prisoners complained that debtors were subsidised by the county to the same bread ration, when they could afford to pay.

Down the centuries Aylesbury people have witnessed some strange cases, but in the

17th century the court also had jurisdiction over the constables—in 1679 William Welch was ordered to return goods he had thieved from dissenters; in 1683 Thomas Read was found to be unfit to be constable because he was one. Beggars were unpopular—the justices of 1679 determined that any Aylesbury people who 'goe and begge' at inns and elsewhere would be slapped straight into the house of correction, and their names removed from the relief records.

Punishment was simple and nasty: in 1690 Thomas Walton did himself no good at all pleading guilty to the theft of a sheep worth 11d from Thomas Folluatt. He was ordered to be whipped at the tail of a cart 'from the Gaole doore to the George signe post' and back again, until his body 'bee bloudy.'

Twenty shillings was a lot of money—and Edward Hadgood was so fined for 'nott sellinge a full quart of strong beer for a penny'. In 1683 the justices were hard on the drinking classes: Simon Goodwin was in trouble for keeping a 'disordered Strong water shoppe' and Thomas Sheene for 'drinkinge strong waters on the Lord's day.'

Idleness was frowned upon, for John Colcell, John Miles and Alexander Oliff were reported in 1685 for 'liveing idly out of service, being of able body.' It was not as if there were not good wages to be had—in 1681 a chief bailiff could secure as much as £6 in the Chilterns, and a pound less in the Vale—still the hills were seen to be the more fertile farm-lands. Menservants could earn £4 10s and women £2 10s—while spinners made 4d per day —but had to find their own meat and drink; labourers could earn twice as much and free-masons the highest of all, at 1s 8d a day.

Still there were those who preferred private enterprise. John Money and Henry Niccolls kept illegal fishing nets while Thomas Pratt, Money, and John White were accused of fishing with a 'shovenett' in the common river. Altogether 22 men were brought before the court for so fishing with divers nets and other 'engines' for catching fish.

Planning permission was a court prerogative also—in 1689 Judith and Joseph Rose were reported for building a cottage on the waste ground at the common dunghill, without per-mission. James Brandon was similarly presented for his building efforts at Bakers Lane end.

And helping the helpless was not necessarily acceptable: Mary Jordan faced a fine of 3s 4d for harbouring vagrants that year. Poaching was indictable: as John Gutteridge found out when he shot local pigeons, in 1690. Finally, in 1691 Sir John Pakington lost patience with the enterprising fishermen, and the court indicted John Money among eight who had managed to persuade 1,000 perch, 100 eels, 40 bream, 20 carp, 100 roach, 1,000 gudgeon and divers other fish from his reach of the river. No doubt depressed by his troubles, Money drank at home during Divine service, and that got him into more trouble with the court. His son, naturally distraught, and perhaps taunted by others of his age, joined his father on the wrong side of the law, by assaulting James Hassell—and he too was indicted, in 1692.

Mindful of the costs of running affairs, the court tried to avoid them when Andrew Flower's wife gave birth in gaol—and sought to establish his responsibility, and his North-amptonshire birthplace. Meanwhile that same year of 1693, consumer protests found Thomas Olliffe and William Goldfinch in court for overcharging for groceries.

Insurance matters fell within the court's concern, and Lawrence Oxley was fined two guineas for 'altering his name and Cheating the Country by Collecting money by pre-tended losses by a fire in Walton, when in truth he susteined no damage thereby.'

The courts were used to discipline religious offenders, and to register dissenters' meeting houses, but by the turn of the century religious toleration was increasing, and punishment less; nonetheless Thomas Read, coffee house keeper, was brought to court for having 'severall dangerous Pamphletts' available on his premises. They were burnt in the Market Place and he was told off and to refrain from taking in such scandalous papers again. Sarah Smith took advantage of his undoubted disarray and found herself arraigned for stealing his linen sleeves.

While fines for swearing were commonplace, 1703 saw a neat twist with Thomas Stratford fined for one oath, William Coaxhead, William Goldsworth and Thomas Chilton fined for two, and Francis Woodcock fined for no less than four—Woodcock was the under keeper at the gaol!

In 1706 a gang of deerstealers was arrested; it transpired they were simply hungry, for William Chandler confessed he had killed a deer in Hartwell Park, taken it home, and shared it with the others accused.

Next year, a truant apprentice Stephen Footman, was whipped by the bridewell keeper and returned to his master Michael Ginger; in 1708 Alexander Olliffe, a long standing county servant, or so he claimed, was run down by a cart when attending a previous court—to add insult to injury the cart contained prisoners. He had been disabled, and 'ever since layne under the chirurgeon's hands att great charges to his utter ruine'. He was granted five pounds. A year later saw Elizabeth Bennett in court for shoplifting linen from a fair stall, and 98-year-old Elizabeth Miles complaining that after 60 years' local residence her allowance of 15d a week only provided heat for her old bones, while Elizabeth Franklyn had the year before been successful in securing a bastardy order against her lover, only to be committed to the bridewell for hard labour as a 'very lewd woman'. To complete the quartet of Elizabeths, in 1711 Elizabeth Goldsworth had two illegitimate children; one died, but the other she charged was fathered by a prisoner—and she was again pregnant, so could not attend court. She subsequently appeared, was discharged, married a seaman, lost touch with him, had a child by another man, who bribed her to blame a third. . . .

In later years sensational trials were eagerly anticipated by the townspeople, who thronged the courts, and as often looked forward to the public executions. In 1823 their most bloodthirsty yearnings must have been sated by the murder of old Needle, the turnpike keeper. In January, Wyatt's coach, known as the old Despatch, left town at 7 am while the frost was still laying. At the first turnpike gate the coachman missed Edward Needle, who usually stood by for the coach. Wyatt went into the lodge and found Needle dead with head wounds, and his wife Rebecca dead in her bedroom. Two gypsies Randall and Croker were soon apprehended and found to have Needle's silver watch and 4s. They had apparently broken into the lodge looking for the week's tolls, usually up to £4, but they were too late for the tolls had been paid over to the lessees. They murdered the Needles with a hurdle. They were both hanged at Aylesbury.

In 1850 Aylesburians were cheated of their entertainment when bank clerk Stratton absconded with £1,068 from Aylesbury Savings Bank. He fled to America, saying he would rather die than be arrested.

One of the most famous trials was that of John Tawell, a respectable married Quaker of Berkhamsted, who murdered one Sarah Hart of Salt Hill, at one time his first wife's servant and later his mistress and mother of his two bastard children, before he became a prominent citizen of Berkhamsted and remarried. Tawell was hanged in Aylesbury Square, before a crowd of 10,000.

Lesser cases throw some light on the times: September 15, 1821, magistrate Col Brown sent two men to the House of Correction for seven days for neglecting their work, and in 1823 a man was whipped three times for defacing an oak tree.

In 1842 a boy was gaoled for four months for stealing apples, worth ½d. On February 26, 1823 when Judge Garrow was escorted by the High Sherriff into town, a contemporary commentator wrote: 'a great concourse of people here as it was likely to be what some folks call a "jolly assizes"; trials for murder, horse stealing, house breaking, and every delicacy of the kind, and lots to be hung.'

This was the year of the Needle case, and the execution after conviction of Banks and two Cribbs for horse stealing. Croker and Randall were hanged two days after their conviction—on the 6th of March 1823, on 'the new drop in front of the County Hall.' The crowd extended out of sight of the gallows; Croker said 'God bless you all' and there was a great snowfall. On March 21 Banks and the Cribbs were hanged—for stealing one horse, worth £7. Yet in May of that same year another horse thief was reprieved—after confessing to the stealing of 30 horses.

Two years later public excitement was at fever pitch over the Whaddon Chase murder; Charlie Lynn and Abraham Hogg were poaching, when Lynn mistook Hogg for a keeper, swung round and in a fit of temporary insanity hit him with the butt of his gun, killing him instantly. Lynn's friends successfully spent £200 on his defence, and he was found not guilty through insanity. Wrote a commentator: 'People say we shall all be killed in our beds if murderers get off like this.' The prison wall acquired a couplet: 'If you have done murder and wish to get clear, Take care and be tried in Buckinghamshire'. So did the pavement:

> 'J. Gibbs has got for sale
> The drop in front of the County Gaol.'

In those days the prisoners swept the streets after Market Day—and collected sweets, tobacco and jokes from passers-by and relatives. Even so, Polly Blatt made a living in the 1820's supplying prisoners through a small trapdoor with anything from tobacco to food—and even the occasional aid to escape—as long as they could pay. Best of all, subject only to their credit rating, prisoners could obtain as much beer as they could get down, and one day in 1831, 112 quarts were conveyed from the White Hart's cellars to the gaol. Charlie Lynn, the Whaddon Chase murderer, chalked up 1s 4d a day, and died of natural causes many years later, judged insane, yet fit enough to quaff his daily pint.

Polly was in difficulties in 1829 for supplying a bag of peas to a prisoner, one Popper-on, for the bag just happened to also contain watch springs, saws, a knife handle, and some nails—'Very dangerous implements for prisoners.' The Sheriff said he would still pay Polly 2s for supplying the prisoners, but she no longer had direct access.

Aylesbury's first regular police force commenced operations following a decision by the Inspectors of Lighting and Watching to introduce three of them 'to guard the town night and day' on December 2, 1837.

In the 1840's the constables were often incapable, and in one case, the constable was both incapable and drunk. His prisoner took himself to gaol. Another constable fell asleep in the 'public' and woke to find his prisoner gone, and the cuffs on him. The County Police Force was instituted in 1857.

An Act had been passed for the building of the gaol in 1737, and by 1823 the treadmill was proving less of a benefit than a danger. That year a prisoner stepped out of the mill and was crushed against the upright post that carried the wheel. In 1832 a prisoner in charge of the mill was killed accidentally by the wheel. In 1833 the accounts showed running costs of the gaol at £2,044 13s. In 1841 the court decided to discontinue use of the treadmill due to two fatalities and four serious injuries.

In 1845 the gaol was the subject of a whitewashing exercise by the Visiting Justices, acting on an adverse report by the Inspector of Prisons, following allegations of indiscipline, and one of the several treadmill accidents. They asserted the victim had disobeyed orders and his injuries were his own fault. Another complaint of illtreatment to a prisoner John Jones drew sharp comments that he was 'refractory' and 'turbulent' and that it took four turnkeys to restrain him. The Justices disagreed that another prisoner had been wrongly forced to clean the Governor's boots. They grandly called for a government enquiry.

In 1846 the gaol was rebuilt, and included 220 common cells, six dark or punishment cells for men, 27 cells for women and 22 rooms in the debtors' section—all modelled on Pentonville. A year later the County Court opened.

In 1877 the Government bought the gaol, enlarged it in 1894 and converted it to a women's prison in 1895. In 1903 a reformatory for drunks was added and by 1915 it was a female Borstal. Today the one-time prison is HM Youth Custody Centre.

The courts that still sit in the county town are the Petty Sessions sitting in the new Magistrates' Court building, behind Walton Street, and the Crown Court, which deals with Quarter Sessions — the Assizes were discontinued in 1972.

The court house itself suffered a major disaster in 1970 when it was seriously damaged by fire, but subsequently restored. Possibly the most famous case of this century was heard there —the Great Train Robbery, involving theft from the night mail in August 1963. A total of over £2m. was stolen, and repercussions of that case still echo through the newspapers of the land as the culprits variously have escaped, been caught, allowed to rot in the Latin American sunshine, moved to top security prisons, and as the years pass, once again return to their freedom.

County Hall, 1845.

ABOVE : HM Prison, built 1845. (Hayward Parrott)
LEFT : County Hall, home to the courts, earlier this century.
RIGHT : 1863 policeman in Spring Gardens. (Osterfield)
BELOW : Chain-gang chains from Aylesbury prison.
(County Museum)

ABOVE: The treadwheel, condemned in 1841. (Osterfield)

BELOW: Go to gaol! 1767 style. (County Record Office)

66

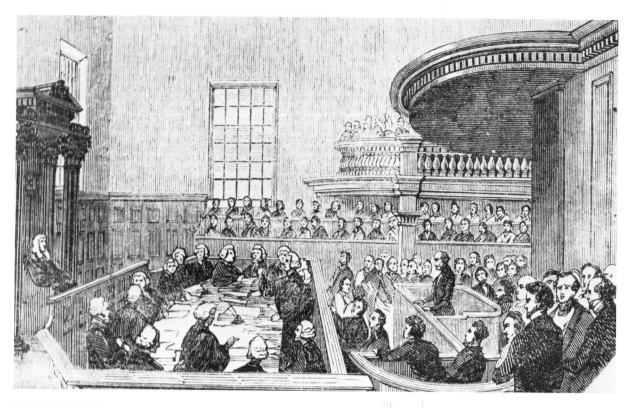

ABOVE: John Tawell faces the judge in Aylesbury's courthouse.
(County Museum)

BELOW: The jury in 1863. (County Museum)

ABOVE: Gentlemen of the constabulary, earlier this century. (Osterfield)

BELOW: The Courthouse, after the 1970 conflagration. (Osterfield)

Graft and Government

Aylesbury town enjoyed some privileges outside the jurisdiction of the Lords of the Manor as far back as Norman times, but there is little evidence of distinctive borough status until the 16th century. The town's site as a junction of routes through the county gave it the edge over other towns, and may have encouraged an early trade in cloth; by the 13th century the townspeople were moving towards some independence, but the power of the local lords put a stop to that once the manor passed out of the Crown's hands. There are late 12th century references to the 'commonalty' of Aylesbury but from 1298 until 1554 the town had no burgess representation in Parliament. From the 14th century there are documentary references to some form of borough status having existed in the 12th century. In 1316 Aylesbury is given in the return of boroughs.

It was in that same century that the men of the town flexed their corporate muscles, and clashed with their lords over pasturage rights. In the 1380s the 'bailiffs and good men' of Aylesbury were granted rights to build and maintain bridges. A 1204 charter for a fair was confirmed in 1439 together with a second fair originally granted in 1239.

But it was in 1450 that the town began to accelerate towards a semblance of independent government with the formation of the Gild of St Mary.

The Gild had some control over the town's affairs. Chief among its leaders were the Baldwins. The Gild acquired land and houses and maintained almshouses, and owned the chapel of St John the Baptist. By 1507 it was represented in the prebendal manor court. In 1499 thirty-two representatives complained about lack of records, of a moot hall for the lord's court and of various other facilities and asked for confirmation of their liberties. They struggled throughout that century and the next for rights of pasturage and for the acquisition of markets and fairs. But when the Baldwins acquired the manor in 1538 the Gild found itself up against the very family of its founders, and inevitably in 1547 the Gild was suppressed. It looked as if the town was once more to be dominated by the manorial system.

But in 1553/4 Aylesbury received its first charter of incorporation. Loyalty to Queen Mary during the quarrels over the succession after Edward VI's death, was rewarded, and the townspeople gained a corporation with bailiff, aldermen and burgesses in common council, with a court of record for pleas of debt, a weekly market and the two fairs they had sought to acquire so long before. They also gained the right to return two members of Parliament. Thus Aylesbury found its feet.

It was not to last long. Sir Thomas Pakington was not happy. The charter was in direct conflict with his rights, real and assumed. The burgesses 'durst not make use of it' and Pakington, taking offence, promptly enclosed the common land pastures, while soon after in 1572 his widow Dorothy took upon herself the right to provide the town's Parliamentary representatives. In 1579 her son obtained the fair rights. In 1586 Lady Dorothy's second husband and another relative, Smith, was 'elected'.

So the town's freedom from manorial domination was shortlived. But this reverse in fact sealed the fate of the feudalists, for with the advent of the Civil War the town was far from Royalist, and the Pakingtons lost their lands and their privileges until the Restoration when Parliamentary representation stayed with the town.

Thenceforth Aylesbury was in a sense two towns—the one that had little or no control over its own affairs while the powerful landowners saw to it that they retained the lion's share of market and fair incomes, leaving purely domestic affairs of vestry and kindred matters of mainly welfare to the ordinary people, and the one that sent its own members to Parliament.

In 1771 the landowners moved in once again on common lands, with wholesale enclosures under the Act, and the awards of 1772.

The Prebendal Estate enclosed 272 acres, with the Vicar adding another 67; Sir Herbert Perrott Pakington Bt enclosed another 438, and altogether 1,740 acres were enclosed. The Lees obtained the turnpike rights for 7 years, after which these were revert to the Prebendal estate; the Verneys, Earl Litchfield (a Pakington connection), Charles Lowndes, Lord Ledespenseur and the Trustees of Bedford's, of Harding's Charities and of Bierton Poor were among others to benefit.

Roads became private and even the verges went over to the landowners. They also gained some obligations, the Commissioners overlooking one item, and having to insert a direction by Royal command that Lee and Pakington between them had to maintain the brook leading to Haydon Mill: 'by sufficient mounding, Fencing, cleansing Scouring be forthwith made and for ever hereafter maintained and kept a good and sufficient fence by and at the expense of the said Sir Herbert Perrott Pakington and his heirs.' That was in 1774.

Individuals were directed to pay compensation in lieu of tithes, one sixty foot highway was marked out for use as a public highway, leading from Aylesbury–Bicester turnpike to Haydon Mill, but the road which 'hath time immemorially been used by the Inhabitants of Quarrendon' on the Earl's estate was to become a private roadway. The footpath from the Thame turnpike over certain allotments remained as a 'publick footway' for 'all his Majesty's Liege Subjects'. Pakington's convenience was studied by an arbitrary exchange of lands at Brook Farm. The lucky proprietors faced £102 expenses for fencing; other fences and drainage cost them £1,542 5s 1¼d. Thomas Tayler was paid £360 3s 6d for putting up the boundary fencing.

The vexatious conflicts between town and lord were eventually resolved with the acquisition of the market by a private company in 1864 from whom the town acquired the rights in 1901.

So while Aylesbury's first burgesses, Thomas Smith and Henry Peckham had a short lived career in the 1550s, and in 1572 Queen Elizabeth, granddaughter of Sir Thomas Boleyn, once Lord of Aylesbury, pushed her own supporters from the county into Parliament, the Pakingtons put up their own man for the town, and by 1586 still held the monopoly of parliamentary representation. Their hold loosened, though there remained family connections with varying members until 1624 when Sir John Pakington was elected: 'the hopes of Aylesbury' whose father had obtained for him a baronetcy when he was still a youth.

In 1625 the bailiffs and burgesses elected Sir Robert Carr and in 1627 Sir Edmund Verney was returned by 350 inhabitants and burgesses of the town. Sir John Pakington and Ralph

Verney were returned in 1640, the latter handing to posterity the first ever report of a debate in the House. He was expelled in 1645 along with Pakington, both accused of Royalist sympathies.

Mayne of Dinton Hall and Scott, who acquired the Pakington estate for £5,000 and rose to power as a major figure in Cromwell's administration, took over.

Henry Phillips spoke for Aylesbury in the Long Parliament, and the Lees took up the burden in the 1660s, with Thomas Lee of Hartwell — the fourth of his family to stand. His partner Ingoldsby was a regicide who escaped the King's wrath by claiming that Cromwell forced him to sign Charles I's death warrant, unlike Thomas Scott, who died in 1660, a traitor's death. The other Aylesbury regicide, Simon Mayne, languished in the Tower, dying of natural causes six months later. Lee was knighted, and Ingoldsby, who married his mother, was made a baronet.

Meanwhile the county elections of 1679 were contested by Lord Wharton and John Hampden as the popular candidates. The establishment, in the person of the Sheriff, tried to foil their ambition by summarily moving the hustings to Buckingham at short notice. The ploy failed. Not long after that a similar upheaval in 1685 saw the election moved to Newport Pagnell—a move masterminded by the infamous Bloody Jeffreys. Wharton and colleague won again—largely due to local indignation, not at all taken in by the ruse of their opponents.

Back in the town elections in 1688, Lee's son, another Sir Thomas, was successful, and on his death in 1691 Mayne, son of the regicide Simon, put up and again in 1695 when he failed. He petitioned to reverse the decision without success, and the town saw a succession of such petitions henceforth, and the disputes which were to bedevil Aylesbury political representation flared up with a succession of failures for Wharton's nominees, in 1698 and Mayne's defeat in 1701. At that time the Borough excluded Walton, and the vote was in the hands of householders and 'Potwallopers'—those who had basic cooking facilities albeit they were fairly lowly tenants. There was no electoral roll, so when Matthew Ashby voted, the returning officers queried his eligibility. He voted for Mayne and Lee, but not for the third candidate, Herbert. His vote rejected, he sued for £200 and at Bucks Summer Assizes he was awarded £5. The defendant returning officers moved for a reversal in the Court of Kings Bench, pleading this was a matter for the House of Commons only, and a majority of three to one judges found no cause for such action: which meant Ashby was back to square one.

Not for the first time the Lords disagreed, and found for Ashby. The Commons riposted with a declaration that anyone challenging the electoral officials was guilty of a breach of privilege.

Meanwhile others were accusing the returning officers of conniving to manage the elections, and in 1703 there were five more Ashby-style actions. The House lost patience. The five were committed to Newgate. Mead, Ashby's attorney would have gone too, only he disappeared. They applied for Habeas Corpus, but the House took custody of them and ignored the writs. The judges concerned granted the latter, and the prisoners petitioned to the Lords for a writ of error. The Lords protected the plaintiffs so the Commons petitioned the Queen! The Lords met the Commons with no constructive result.

Both sought Royal backing. The Queen tactfully dismissed Parliament, the prisoners were liberated and the story ended with Aylesbury men fighting for their rights and incidentally breaking up the government of the day. Aylesbury people were not amused: at the 1705 election stones were thrown at the candidates with the shouts: 'Knock them on the head; beat the rogues' brains out.'

In 1714 one of Aylesbury's representatives was Sir Nathanial Mead—brother of Robert Mead, Ashby's attorney, and forebear of the wife of John Wilkes—Jack of Aylesbury.

Wilkes was born in 1727 and died 70 years later. He was first elected for Aylesbury in 1757, by agreement taking Thomas Potter's seat. He had been partly educated at Aylesbury and married into an Aylesbury family by wedding Miss Mead and settling at the Prebendal House. His first act was to unsuccessfully contest a northern seat; he then became High Sheriff in 1754, and a year later a Feoffee of the Aylesbury Grammar School. Letters survive which show how Wilkes set about securing his seat by enquiring the cost of securing votes. Charles Lowndes proposed 3 gns a head. Wilkes also had to fix the incumbent, by arranging an alternative government appointment. The whole deal cost him £7,000 but he was returned unopposed.

By 1762 Wilkes was on the threshold of his historic stand. Lord Bute, Head of the Treasury organised a weekly scandal sheet called The Briton—a sort of Private Eye in reverse. Wilkes countered with The North Briton, to which Bute opposed a third paper, The Auditor. The original and last papers died but Wilkes' paper survived, and in 1763 he published some notes on the King's Speech which caused grave offence in the corridors of power.

The Secretary of State for the Home Dept issued a writ for the arrest of all concerned, including Wilkes. He was duly arrested, and applied for Habeas Corpus. He had influential friends, for Earl Temple was the man behind the application. It did no good. Wilkes was deliberately shifted four times in a half day to evade the writ, and ended up in the Tower. On May 3 1763 he was brought before the bar of the Court of Common Pleas. He was remanded to the Tower, but this time his friends had proper access. After his second appearance at the Court on May 6, his arrest was declared illegal and he was released.

Steps were taken by the establishment to displace Temple and Wilkes from county appointments, but this did not stop them suing for damages, both for Wilkes and the others involved in the original arrests. It cost the wrongdoers dear and Wilkes secured £1,000 damages. It also established finally the illegality of arbitrary arrest.

On November 15, the House considered the relevant 45th issue of the North Briton that caused the original fuss, and found it to be seditious. It was ordered to be burnt. The result was pandemonium. The City mob attacked the Sheriff and the hangman, rescued the paper and raised the famous cry 'Wilkes and Liberty!'

Wilkes then addressed the House somewhat indiscreetly, and offered to waive his privilege as a member should they confirm it, and go before a jury in the matter.

That was not the only scene of his drama, for he found himself challenged by individuals who felt themselves personally maligned by his scandal sheet. His moonlit duel with Earl Talbot caused little harm, but he was badly wounded by Mr Martin in Hyde Park. In December he travelled to France to recover and to let the furore die down. He was expelled from the House in his absence, and so Aylesbury lost its representative and liberty its champion. The Lords outlawed him for not being present to hear the House condemn his paper as libellous and blasphemous.

Ignoring his outlawry, Wilkes returned in 1768 and contested a seat for the City. He failed, then tried for Middlesex and won. But on April 27 he was arrested. The mob had not forgotten their hero; they rescued him but he gave himself up again. On May 10, a mob gathered again and escorted the prisoner to Westminster and a riot began. Seven died from the soldier's response. Wilkes' popularity knew no bounds and £20,000 were raised in his defence. Aylesbury's electorate wrote to tell their members to support Wilkes in the House. 1,800 freeholders of the county petitioned in his favour, and on June 8 his outlawry was reversed, he received short prison sentences and fines, and he was expelled from his recently won seat. The electors re-elected him at no expense, but this was deemed void. Wilkes tried a third time, won handsomely, and was unseated again by the House's decision. At this the country fermented at the lack of respect for electoral choice. In the following November, the original case for wrongful arrest and seizure of papers resulted in Wilkes' victory and £4,000 damages award. In 1770 he was released, and returned in 1774 for Middlesex; in 1780 he was again returned, and in 1782 the House by a majority cleared his name. He retired in 1790.

It was clear even when Wilkes was proclaiming rights and liberties that the fundamental right we take for granted was a matter of money. Candidates in the 18th century would offer up to twelve guineas and other gifts to voters, even to the extent that landlords would not press for rental payments until after an election. Candidates would push up the ante, leapfrogging each other's bribes. In 1802 matters came to a head. This was 'Bent's election'. It promised to be a quiet affair, but the potwallopers wanted none of it. Quiet elections were not profitable ones. They determined to 'open the borough'. Bribery was brought right out into the open, and even the town crier advertised how much and where the 'gifts' were. By getting up three candidates, the voters of Aylesbury saw to it that some 10,000 guineas were available for the taking. Bent was the third man selected as a candidate. He had £3,500 to spend. On average each vote earnt nine guineas. The nominations were made on a tombstone, and polling was at County Hall. Bent came second, but a petition was lodged against his return, not least because of the duplication of votes for him and the other successful candidate.

The House of Commons appointed a Select Committee, who completed a 200 page report, as a result of which Bent was out, and found guilty of bribery. Witnesses agreed that there were two bowls at each inn—one held punch, the other guineas. You had a glass of one and three of the other.

The number of voters who ate at one inn alone totalled 759 though only 420 actually cast their votes. One day's dinner for voters and others concerned included 20 dishes of fish, 10 dishes of boiled fowls, 10 dishes of roast fowls, 1 boiled leg of pork and peaspudding, 2 boiled hams, 2 haunches of mutton, 6 geese, 10 pigeon pies, 3 dishes of boiled beef, 3 dishes of roast beef, 2 fillets of veal, 1 loin of veal, 2 roast legs of pork, 2 forequarters of lamb, 2 dishes of roast turkey, 1 dish of boiled turkey, 2 dishes of roast pigs, 16 plum puddings, 60 custard puddings, 20 fruit pies, 10 dishes of custards, fruit, blancmange, jellies, etc. This merely represented the 'headquarters' fare for the followers of one candidate at the White Hart.

In 1804 Aylesbury exercised the House, as well it might for this latest example of unruliness. The borough was nearly disfranchised, but in the event, the House decided to set off the potwallopers by extending the vote—to include those who held a 40 shilling freehold and the county vote. This doubled the electorate from 450 to 1,000.

Actions were started against those involved, amounting to £1m.

There is little doubt the Black Act, as the potwallopers dubbed it, had the desired effect, but it did not entirely eradicate the effect abundant funds had on the outcome. The new freeholders had to reach the hustings, and doubtless candidates paid for their expenses.

In addition, freeholders with relevant holdings multiplied. Hartwell was speedily split up to yield 52 new votes for the benevolent candidate, from the tenantry, the vote passing onto the successor tenant!

In 1806 Lt Gen Sir George Nugent and George Henry Compton Cavendish opened the new order as members of Aylesbury. In 1814 Charles Compton Cavendish, later to become Lord Chesham, was elected. In 1818 William Rickford, who has left his name on the town, succeeded and Nugent was second. Cavendish dropped to third place. In 1820 Rickford and Nugent were elected.

At the 1826 election the 'publics' gave open house, and 'every one inclined to get drunk had an opportunity to do so.' In 1828, Rickford warned the House against transferring the bribery from one class of voters to another.

In 1831 the borough and county elections were held together and there was a considerable contest. Nugent and Rickford won Aylesbury. Lord Kirkwall was David to Nugent's Goliath. But he lost. The Reform Bill of that year changed the system again, substantially enlarging the franchise

Col Hamner, candidate in 1832, complained to printer Woodman of a scurrilous poster he had printed. He got a black eye for his troubles—consisting of printer's ink. Said a contemporary reporter: 'They won't go into a printing office again for a good while, I'll warrant.'

When elections for the borough were due in the 1850's, the Hartwell Gooseberry Society was held at the Bugle—under the auspices of the teetotal chairman Dr Lee. Much bribery still went on under cover at this gathering from afar of many of the independent electors. Hartwell House was thrown open, and the meetings lasted from noon to late at night. Joe Carter, landlord of the Bugle received compensation from the good Doctor for loss of business, when in reality he was restocking with Aylesbury beer daily after his own nut brown ale was exhausted by the visitors to the great 'temperance festival.'

By 1852 party politics took over, Richard Bethell, Solicitor General and later knighted, sat for Aylesbury in the '50's, and in 1865 one of the new lords was elected—a Rothschild. The 1872 Ballot Act finally finished the 'good old days.'

Locally, in 1849 the Board of Health was appointed, precursor to the later Urban District Council. In 1857 the watch passed to the newly formed county police. The watch had earlier in 1825 prohibited Sunday trading—a practice more general in Aylesbury than elsewhere. The Fire Brigade came under the Board of Health—previously fires had ravaged the town in 1669, 1750 and 1765.

In the early 1800s the amount of poor rate was actually reduced marginally but by 1818 it had crept up to nearly £5,000. In 1839 the new Workhouse was erected in Mill Close, and the year after, when the Reform Act was passed, 90 Aylesbury men were on relief.

The Bucks County Council held their first meeting in 1889, and the Board of Health their last on December 17, 1894; the new Urban District Council came to power December 31 that year. And on January 1, 1917, the Borough of Aylesbury was reborn with a new Charter of Incorporation.

On March 31, 1974 Aylesbury lost its separate status and its Borough with the local government reorganisation. The Borough and the District Council, together with those for Buckingham and the Rural Districts of Winslow and of Wing were all merged into the new Aylesbury Vale District Council. The Charter Trustees succeeded the Borough with responsibility for the Borough arms, so that these still survived, and the town still had a Mayor.

Voces suas tam affirmativas quam negativas cetaq omia et singla tum faciant et exequnt
que aly burgenses vel alius burgens parliamenti nri q quibuscunq alys burges aut alio
Burgo quocunq hent faciunt et exequunt aut habere facere aut exequi valeant seu
possunt racoe aut modo quocunq

Volumus etiam ac per pntes concedimus pfat ballio aldermanns
et burgensibz dci burgi de Ailesbury q heant et hent has lras patentes sub
magno Sigillo nro Anglie debito modo fact et sigillat absq fine seu feodo
magno vel parvo nobis in hanaperio nro seu alibi ad usum nrm proinde quoqn
reddend solvend seu faciend

Eo qd expressa mentio de vero valore anuo aut certitudine pmissor
sive eor alicuius aut de alys donis siue concessionibz per nos vel q aliquem
pgenitorum morm prefatis ballio aldermanns et burgensibz burgi pdci
ante hec tempa fact in presentibz minime fact existit aut aliquo
Statuto actu ordinacoe prouisione seu restriccoe in contrarui fact
edit ordinat seu prouis aut aliqua alia re causa vel materia quacunq
in aliquo non obstante

A copy made at the time of the 1554 Charter of Incorporation granted by
Queen Mary. (Bucks Archaeological Society)

75

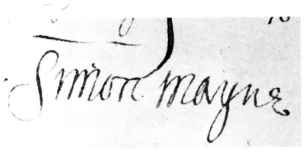

ABOVE LEFT: Simon Mayne's signature. (Osterfield)

ABOVE RIGHT: John Wilkes 1727-1797. (Margaret Sale)

BELOW LEFT: Wilkes' fame gave the Derby craftsmen a theme for 1780.
(County Museum)

BELOW RIGHT: The mob rescue Wilkes. (Osterfield)

Hogarth's view of Wilkes. (County Museum)

Refolved,

That it appears to this Committee, that fuch a notorious Syftem of Corruption was formed, and fuch Inftances of individual Acts of Bribery were committed, previous to the faid Election, with a View to influence the fame, as to render it incumbent on the Committee to fubmit the fame to the moft ferious Confideration of the Houfe, in order that fuch Proceedings may be inftituted thereon, as the Houfe in its Wifdom may think proper to adopt.

TO THE
POTWALLOPERS
OF
Aylesbury.

Potwallopers all! ye mere skum of the earth!
   Pray attend to the compliment paid you;
And vote for the man, with your votes little worth,
   Who has publicly dar'd to upbraid you.

Shout aloud for Reform---let the Whigs have
    their will,
   Tho' your country will long rue the day;
And you'll find to your cost that you've gain'd by
    the Bill,
   Just as much as *some noble Lords pay.*

Elect as your Member this *liberal* Peer,
   Whom you hear with such kindness determine,
That, unless you are rated at ten pounds a-year,
   You deserve to be swept off like vermin.

[*May, Printer, Aylesbury.*]

David & Goliath.

Goliath of Gath, that vain boaster of old,
   Who the armies of Israel defied;
By a stripling, in virtue and fortitude bold,
   Was struck to the dust in his pride.

The *Goliath of Bucks*, like his prototype, wear
   As his head piece some talents of *brass*,
And with equal presumption and arrogance swea
   That he'll trample his foes like the grass.

But though this huge Giant, so fierce and so b
   Protests that in pieces he'll hack us;
For his threats and his stature we'll not care a
   With our own little David to back us.

[*May, Printer, Aylesbury.*]

ABOVE: The 1804 Select Committee reports. (County Record Office)

BELOW: In 1831 Kirkwall (David) challenged Nugent (Goliath) for the potwallopers' vote in the Reform Bill contest. (John Francis)

To the
ELECTORS
OF THE
Borough & Hundreds of
AYLESBURY.

GENTLEMEN.

Notwithstanding "*the entire Confidence*" Lord Nugent feels in himself, and the "*entire Defiance and Contempt*" he has been pleased to express towards me and my Friends, the State of the Poll this day, and the numerous Promises I have received, induce me to continue the contest with unabated ardour and every prospect of success. Thanking you for your kind exertions and good wishes,

I have the Honour to be,
GENTLEMEN,
Your very obedient humble Servant,
KIRKWALL.

Aylesbury, May 6th, 1831.

STATE OF THIS DAY'S POLL.
Mr. Rickford . . **178**
Lord Nugent . . **111**
Viscount Kirkwall . **82**

MAY, PRINTER, AYLESBURY.

LEFT: Kirkwall keeps trying. (Bucks Archaeological Society)

RIGHT: Richard Dighton produced this View of Nugent in 1822. (Mansell Collection)

B.

R B.

Buck...hy To the Churchwardens and Overseers of the Poor of the *Parish* — — of *Aylesbury* in the said *County*

BY Virtue of an Order of his Majesty's Justices of the Peace in and for the said *County* in their general Quarter Sessions assembled, you are hereby required in thirty Days Time from your Receipt of this Precept, or otherwise having had due Notice thereof, to pay to me, out of the Money by you collected, or to be collected for the Relief of the Poor, the Sum of *7:9"0* — — being the Proportion of your said *Parish* — — for and towards the general County Rate, for the repairing of Bridges; repairing of the Goal, and for the Relief of Prisoners therein; and for the Relief of the Prisoners in the *King's-Bench* and *Marshalsea* Prisons; repairing and furnishing the House of Correction, with the Salary of the Keeper thereof; the Treasurer's Salary; the Coroner's Fees; the Charges concerning Vagrants, Soldiers, Carriages, convicting and transporting Felons, and other County Charges. And herein you are not to fail on the Peril that shall ensue thereof. GIVEN under my Hand at *Aylesbury* in the said *County* the *22* — — — — Day of *April* in the Year of our Lord *1766.*

Robt. Paten -High Constable.

N:B:
*Be please to bring the above
Sum to my House in Aylesbury
the 26th day of May next 1766:*

Sold by J COLES, Stationer, in Fleet-Street.

1766 rate demand. (County Record Office)

AYLESBURY WATCHING AND LIGHTING.

WANTED---For Sunday next, the 19th instant, about
FORTY SMALL ACTIVE BOYS,
to bear Torches or Lanthorns in all the principal thoroughfares
leading to the

CHURCH,

and other places of Worship, both before and after Evening
service.

Application to be made to me personally, on, or before, Wednesday next,
H. HAYWARD,

Secretary to the Oil Lamp Inspectors.

N. B.---The terms are **3d.** for each Boy, and **6d.** for those
finding their own LIGHTS. The appointment may probably
last some months. **WANTED ALSO FOR HIRE** some Second-
hand Lanthorns.

Churchyard, Aylesbury, Jan. 13, 1840.

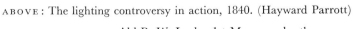

ABOVE: The lighting controversy in action, 1840. (Hayward Parrott)

CENTRE LEFT: Ald R. W. Locke, 1st Mayor under the
second Charter, 1917. (Osterfield)

CENTRE: The firemen of Aylesbury. (Margaret Sale)

BELOW: Aylesbury's MP in the 1850's—Richard Bethell.
(Margaret Sale)

ABOVE: The old Market House of Henry VIII's time.

LEFT TO RIGHT: 13th century cooking pot from Buckingham Street,

17th century Bellarmine jug from Overton Road, and 13th century jug.
(County Museum)

CENTRE: In the small change famine of the 17th century, a local trader
struck this halfpenny token. (All County Museum)

A Celebrate Market

'The towne selfe of Aylesbury standeth on an hill in respect of all the ground thereabout, a 3 mile flatt north from Chiltern Hilles. The town is meetly well builded with tymbre, and in it is a celebrate market. It standeth in the high-waye from Banbury to London, and Buckingham to London.' Thus Leland in the time of Henry VIII. Leland summed up Aylesbury with all economy. It is a crossroads, and that brought it trade. Backed by the Vale, and its agricultural output, the town was bound to favour a market.

The Romano-British settlers in and around Aylesbury probably established the first trading as such — in cloth. The Saxon mint indicated the growing importance of Aylesbury as a trading centre; then the Norman survey suggests that trade had declined by the 11th century.

With Aylesbury 'terra regis' the royal party in all probability hunted in the vicinity when journeying to the Midlands. At that time the Vale was a good deal damper than now, but Bernwood Forest was adjacent, and without doubt Bucks' most important reserve for hart and boar. The Norman kings extended the forest area, inherited from the Saxon lords, and increased the severity of forest laws — there are plenty of references to the effect on Aylesbury, especially on wrongdoers found at Whaddon, the nearest wooded tract to the settlement. Bernwood was not a forest in modern terms, but a waste tract with plenty of cover for the quarry.

But it was the market that made Aylesbury: gradually the stalls in the middle became shops, houses and inns, closing off Market Square from Kingsbury Square—the two once forming a continuous congress for commerce, Kingsbury itself the original site for the earliest markets.

The Market Hall was rebuilt in 1530, and the Kings Head dates from 1569, though what remains today is of 17th century origin. Spittle (hospital) mill traces its ancestry back to 1477. There were two mills in Aylesbury at 1087, but it is unlikely they formed the basis of any industrial trend; Aylesbury's mills were for local use. The main activity remained the working of the land, and by the 1460s corn harvesting paid 11d an acre to the labourer, while dyking brought in 2d less. One profitable sideline was producing livestock pens for the fairs. Most worked the land for others and for themselves.

Some worked on community projects, such as the conduit water supply laid as far back as 1478, though the first private house to be supplied with running water was 230 years ago.

By the 13th century, a fair was established, and then a second. The market tolls formed an important part of the lord's incomes, and were much coveted by the townspeople, actively so in the 16th and 17th centuries.

The Market Hall was demolished in 1802 and another erected by the Marquess of Buckingham. This was demolished in 1866. A new hall was by then up, on the site of the old White Hart—the Corn Exchange—built in 1864 by the Aylesbury Market Co, itself formed the previous year by Act of Parliament, and its rights and duties acquired by the town in 1901.

In fact, Aylesbury has been a crossroads since Romano-British times, attracting trade. That crossroads developed into a market and that formed the nucleus for a community based on trading—a tradition that survived until the last cattle Exchange Street market in 1927, the final Market Square fair in 1938, and the last act by the planners, when they violated the heart of the town in the 1960s, destroyed the living pattern of the original place and built a new modern commercial centre for the second half of the 20th century.

Yet industry is no newcomer. Not far from Aylesbury two staple industries emerged early on. There were brickfields at Claydon in the 17th century, and bricks in 1656 cost 6s a thousand to make and burn. In 1560 all the nation's needles were manufactured at Long Crendon.

Perhaps the very convenience of Aylesbury's site across the routes from London to the Midlands and the scale and richness of the Vale inhibited the development of early industry, or of crafts. There was work enough on the land and in the market. Not that it was always thus. In 1771 agricultural rents in the Vale were between 6s and 20s an acre, and the farming was regarded as 'dirty' according to contemporary Arthur Young. Most of the land was still unenclosed, and worked on the fallow system; there was no underground drainage—an essential for plain farming. Said Young: 'All this vale would make as fine meadows as any in the world' if it was enclosed and drained. As it was, the tenants gathered dung, dried it and burnt it—a primitive approach to natural fertiliser for such a late period. Yet in 1826 Cobbett speaks eloquently of Aylesbury and district, and farming improved with incomes to match into the second half of the 19th century. In 1856, farmworkers were earning as much as 12s a week. Then poor management brought depression to the town and district, with cereal production halved between 1867 and 1904 and as much as half the Vale turned to grass; cattle increased from 57,448 head in 1867 to 75,990 in 1904, but sheep and pigs were much reduced in numbers.

Meanwhile, in 1887 there was a weekly Saturday market, weekly fatstock sale, Wednesday, and six fairs. The Wool Fair was in July, the Fat Cattle Fair in December and the Sale of Rams Fair in August.

Some work was available in the town at least—for the prisoners. A pump was attached to the gaol treadmill in 1825 and water supplied to those who paid. The mains supply took over in 1867.

But one craft had emerged. By the 17th century pillow lace had grown beyond its domestic purpose into a cottage industry. In 1672 workhouse children were taught the rudiments by Mary Sutton, and lace became Aylesbury's staple manufacture—so much so that 19th century candidates for Parliament had to support hand lace-making against the machine age. There was a lace Queen, and the successful candidate's chair for his triumphal procession was covered with lace. It was possible to earn 25s a week at the lace pillow.

In 1787 the importance of the lace industry can be gauged by the first evidence of a gift to workhouse inmates, and in connection with an item of luxury rather than essential nature. The overseers gave 3s to the lacemakers to keep the feast of St Catherine, patron saint of lacemakers.

In 1806 Lyson was able to observe: 'There is no manufacture carried on in this town, excepting that of lace.' But in the late 1820's the machine took Aylesbury's prosperity away to the Midlands where they turned out the new product faster and cheaper, and many of the outworkers were out of work.

In April 1826 it was reported that the lace trade was 'in complete stagnation'. Wages were down from 15s to 2s 6d: 'machine lace is so much cheaper,' and there was 'great poverty.' A year later there was a temporary improvement, but in 1828 the citizens petitioned the King to hold a Court Drawing-room at stated periods, where Bucks lace would be worn to create a fashion. At one time Bucks boasted 150,000 lacemakers. In 1832 a lacemaker was lucky to earn 6d a week. There was a shortlived revival in 1839.

Lacemaking was concentrated at Aylesbury and three other Bucks towns, and it was claimed that the best lace was from Aylesbury. But in the end lace making went into decline, strawplait was the up and coming industry. Aylesbury quickly became one of two main centres in the county—doubtless because the facilities existed for a plait market, essential to this craft, where middlemen were needed to deal in both materials, and end product. In 1813 plait workers could earn 22s a week. In 1846 Robert Thorpe established a new plait market. This traded weekly.

Earlier, in 1828, all workers of straw plait were stretched to fulfil demand, but by 1847 that trade too was in decline.

A wool fair was established in 1833.

Silk took over next. Robert Nixon of Kaye's Tring silk mill, set up a mill in Aylesbury in conjunction with the workhouse overseers—anxious to employ paupers, many of them once lacemakers. The mill in fact was exclusive to paupers, against which the overseers gave £200 towards the buildings, and donated the land. In 1830 there were forty hand looms in operation; in 1844 the mill changed hands, and by 1859 there were 200 employed and the looms were steam powered. By 1885 the number of steam looms had increased to seventy, and a branch had opened at Waddesdon earlier, in 1843. This grew also, to employ forty-two women by 1862—but on handlooms only. There was a smaller mill at Whitchurch. Silk was a major Aylesbury industry by the end of the last century.

Meanwhile, smallholding was growing in one speciality—the Aylesbury duck. Proximity to the London market, and perhaps an accident of breeding provided the succulent young Aylesbury or white ducklings which could be got to town quickly. Walton became a centre for local output, and there are those who can recall the four separate flocks that congregated on Walton Pond, dividing to go their separate ways to the home farms at feeding time.

In 1921 the Aylesbury duckling trade was a speculative one. The birds matured quickly, large as a breed. The Easter market was important and to produce 1,000 birds for the table, a breeder would need 30-40 stock ducks. Food comprised egg, bread, bullock's liver, rice, boiled offal, barley meal and grit. The Aylesbury duckling was prone to disease, and put to market at 8-12 weeks. Carriers called fortnightly. The birds fetched from 6 to 10s each. Fouled ground and feed prices finally eliminated the major profits in the '20s and the Aylesbury duckling went the way of the lace-makers.

Back in 1784 some casual work was to be had, for the overseer's accounts record two or three 'roundsmen' who were unemployed but fit labourers—the following year the number had risen to thirty, costing the parish some £7. There was then, as now, argument as to whether the welfare system encouraged idleness or truly cushioned the poor. Nothing changes. Landlord Richard Gurney refused to pay rates, for he claimed no one would work for him, as they could do better on relief; yet 300 people wanted to lease his corn. Clearly, unemployment was becoming a problem.

General distress among farmers in 1821 was evidenced by poor crops, and worse prices. Landowners returned rents in some cases, and in others reduced them; many landlords deferred the rents indefinitely. Minor disasters included the day Polly Speed of the Bricklayer's Arms was tossed by a cow in the market.

By 1830 unemployment was an epidemic in the area, with local wages rising at half the rate of northern towns, and the overseers faced with some £8,000 expenses annually, an inadequate workhouse and weekly bills for the unemployed alone of £35 and more—by the following year the problem was reducing, with weekly expenses down to half these amounts.

Some idea of earlier meat prices can be gauged from a butcher's account for 1685, with shoulder of mutton at 8d, leg of veal 9d and a haunch of beef at 4s 6d.

In 1829 the rates were a major burden; farmers were giving their tree loppings to the poor and the lords were giving coal. Lord Chandos ordered a lace dress for his wife. The rich in general helped the poor, but the overseers were at their wits' end to support all who were in need. The poor themselves were desperate—even to breaking up mill machinery.

One craft spread the name of the town far afield, and is commemorated in a charity and a town facility. Clockmaking in Aylesbury has its beginnings in John Stone's late 15th century will whereby he gave two tenements for a clock and chimes 'for ever'. In 1691 the churchwardens granted John Aylward a 31 year lease of these cottages at Green End, against his agreement to provide and maintain the clock and chimes. The Trust still owns the property.

A later John Stone made clocks at Aylesbury from 1764 to 1789, and his son succeeded him in the same business. Joseph Cooke followed the same intricate trade in the 1760s. Other 18th century Aylesbury clockmakers included the Neales—Euclid (died 1736), his son James, and Francis; Joseph Quartermaine, and a later Quartermaine employee Thomas White Field—whose business survived until the second decade of this century; John Hill; George Spurr, Joseph Cooke, and at least nine 19th century clockmakers included Frederick Fidelio Lehmann and Neal Campbell. For some 150 years Aylesbury was the county centre of this highly skilled business.

One other craft survived into the 20th century—basketmaking, from local osier beds. The picking and peeling of the osiers made the hands bleed and stained as if shelling walnuts. The work was worth 2d per bundle. The hampers were made at the LMSR basket works in Park Street, for use on the railway. Local osier beds at Lover's Walk and between Exchange Street and the canal supplied the osiers until 1938. The craft died in 1947.

In 1757 there were no printers in Aylesbury, or none recorded. Today printing and publishing is a major activity in the town—a fitting combination of craft and industry. By 1792 there was a print plant and a newspaper—the Buckinghamshire Herald, founded July 28. It moved to Berkhamsted after 18 weeks, and died a year later. Bucks was late to launch its own newspapers. In 1820 the Bucks Chronicle emerged—and died in 1840. In 1824 the Bucks Gazette and Windsor and Eton Express were founded; their Bucks connection ceased in 1849.

The Bucks Chronicle rose phoenix-like in 1848 to survive until 1872 when it was merged with the 'new' Herald, which had been born on January 7, 1832. The Aylesbury News and Advertiser for Bucks was launched December 1, 1836, changed its name ten years later to the Bucks Advertiser and Aylesbury News, but now only the Herald survives today. The Aylesbury Reporter was short lived — from 1880-1906, and Edgar Wallace's Bucks Mail founded in Aylesbury in 1930, even more so; it closed when the novelist was defeated in his candidacy for Mid Bucks in 1931.

In 1867 Hazell Watson & Viney Ltd moved from London, first opening a country branch at California, then moving to the present Tring Road site. Extensions were built in 1885, 1895, 1906, 1907 and 1911, establishing the company as Aylesbury's premier undertaking. In 1920, 1926, 1933 and 1935 further additions and enlargements occurred, followed by club premises and a theatre in 1936, and a new factory in 1937.

Aylesbury diversified in 1870 with the arrival of the Aylesbury Condensed Milk Co, which expanded further in 1899 and was later absorbed by Nestle and in 1885 the bibulous found consolation in the maturing at Aylesbury of sherry from Spain. Printers Hunt Barnard and Co Ltd came to Aylesbury in 1898, occupying a works in Buckingham Street and twenty-nine years later moving to new premises at Milton Road—The Sign of the Dolphin.

The model steam bakers started in Aylesbury in 1889; they are no more. The Aylesbury Brewery Co Ltd took over the Walton Brewery in 1895—there is no longer an indigenous Aylesbury beer, and the Bourton Street Brewery was in fact demolished in 1894.

The Bifurcated and Tubular Rivet Co Ltd, established in 1910 in Aylesbury, made the Iris car after World War One, and the Siva Motor Co linked to BTR through the family Paterson, in the '70s produced the Llama kit car.

In 1966 Aylesbury acquired a brand new market place — the concrete and glass Friars Square — and closed the old one to through traffic. That same year the County Offices monolithic structure rose sheer above the town — a castle to stand in place of the one that maybe never was. Industry spread at Rabans Lane, new courts and District council offices housed justice and administration, a hypermarket came soon after and another in the nineties. A palace of blue glass defies gravity in the shadow of the 'castle' and in 1993 Friars Square acquired new clothes with a classic concourse of shops and stalls and stylish ornament beneath a soaring sky of glass on three floors, newly bridged to the car park and arcaded onto Market Square, once more the centre of street trade. Development continues.

The town's commercial development is readily apparent from a comparison of local directories over a century and a half. Pigot & Co's 1822 entries precede those of Musson and Craven in 1853, and Kelly's of 1899. The 1,974 equivalents are shown last.

Activity	1822	1853	1899	1974
PROFESSIONAL				
Attorneys (Solicitors)	10	10	?	30
Accountants	none	2	1	11
Architects & Surveyors	2	3	6	15
Auctioneers/Estate Agents	4	3	4	4
Banks/bankers	1	4	4	6
Building Societies	none	none	1	9
Chiropodist	none	none	none	1
Insurance agents/ Companies	13	31	3	25
Osteopath	none	none	none	none
Opticians	none	none	none	6
Physicians/Doctors	2	2	8	18
Surgeons		4	3	
(Surgeon) Dentists	none	1	5	16
Vererinary Surgeons	3	3	3	1
Farmers and graziers	?	10	9	10
CRAFTS				
Artificial fly dresser	none	none	1	none
Bird and animal preservers/ Taxidermist	none	2	1	4
Basket and sieve makers	4	3	4	none
Birdcage maker	none	none	1	none
Blacksmiths	5	3	3	none
Bookbinders	1	none	1	1
Printers	3	2	6	7

Activity	1822	1853	1899	1974
Bootmakers	13	30	25	
Boot repairers				2
Braziers and tinplate workers	3	2	1	none
Boat builders	none	none	none	1
Brickmakers	2	3	1	1
Cabinet makers Upholsterers	3	5	6	2
Carpenters	5	3	10	none
		(also builders)		
Joiner	none	4	none	3
Bricklayers	2	1	?	?
Dressmakers/ seamstresses	none	none	26	?
Coachmakers/builders and wheelwrights	5	5	5	1
Coopers	4	5	1	none
Cycle makers	none	none	4	none
Machine maker/ precision engineers etc.	1	1	1	3
Dyer	none	1	1	none
Gasfitter/locksmith	none	none	1	none
Glovers	3	2	none	none
Gunsmiths	2	none	1	none
Hairdressers	8	8	10	26
Lacemakers	2	none	none	none
Milliners	10	18	2	none
Monumental masons	2	1	3	none

Activity	1822	1853	1899	1974
Painters/plumbers/ glaziers	7	11	10	8
Photographers	none	none	2	5
Saddlers	4	4	3	1
Signwriters	none	none	none	1
Stay maker	none	1	none	none
Straw hat makers	4	3	1	none
Tailors	10	17	14	none
Umbrella and parasol maker	none	1	1	none
Watch and clock makers and gold- smiths	2	5	7	none
(Jewellers)	1	1	none	6
Whitesmiths	2	3	none	none
Wire worker	1	none	none	none
Wood turner	1	1	none	none
Ropemaker	1	none	1	none
Hatter	1	3	1	none
Cutler	1	1	none	none
Sawyer	1	none	none	none
Currier/leather cutter/ tanner	1	2	2	none
RETAIL				
Animal feedstuffs	none	none	1	1
Antiques/second-hand	none	none	2	2
Bakers	17	17	22	15

Activity	1822	1853	1899	1974
Beer retailers	none	23	29	none (see wine)
Booksellers	4	8	4	3
Newsagents/stationers				22
Builders' marchants	none	none	1	3
Butchers	13	21	20	15
Furnishers (see cabinet makers)	none	5	10	13
Cattle dealers	9	7	11	none
China/glass	2	3	3	?
Co-operative	none	none	1	1 (4)
Chemists	3	5	4	12
Clothing (exc. dressmakers)	4	5	7	43
Fabrics	6	3	?	9
Flooring contractors	none	none	none	2

Activity	1822	1853	1899	1974
Coal	5	11	13	6
Corn dealers	8	7	10	none
Dairymen	none?	3	10	5
Drapers	none	7	10	none
Stores	none	none	none	3
Fancy goods	none	none	5	3
Gardeners/seedsmen/florists	3	6	9	2
Grocers/tea dealers (inc. cash and carry delicatessen)	8	13	29	35
Cheese/butter/bacon factors	none	none	10	none
Greengrocers	none	none	3	10
Hawkers	none	none	1	none
Hay dealers	none	1	none	none
Horse dealers	none	1	3	none

Activity	1822	1853	1899	1974
Hardware	2	3	4	7
Marine store dealers	none	none	1	none
Musical instrument	none	none	2	1
Marine store dealers	none	none	1	none
Pig dealer	none	none	3	none
Rag and bone	none	2	none	none
Salt	none	1	none	none
General shopkeepers	10	15	25	15
Toys	2	1	?	4
Tobacconists (exc. CTN)	none	1	4	2
Wine and spirit merchants	3	3	7	10
Haberdashers	1	4	?	1
Fishmongers	1	2	5	3
Fried fish	none	none	1	6

Retail activity has changed during the period reviewed. There were (1975) a number of purely modern firms: petshops (3); do-it-yourself shops (3); fuel oil distributors (1); motorcycles (1); electrical (6); credit check traders (3); fishing tackle suppliers (2); motor agents (9); petrol stations (6); model shops (2); glass merchants (2); leathergoods dealers (3); radio/TV dealers and hirers (8); discount stores (3); sports goods suppliers (2); timber merchants (1); tool dealers (2); record shops (3); typewriter agents (2); wallpaper suppliers (3); tyre dealers (5); and take-away food shops (3).

Some of these have clearly replaced the craftsmen of yesteryear, such as the glass merchant and do-it-yourself stores substituting for the carpenters and glaziers.

A comparison of engineers would be pointless, for apart from agricultural engineers, there are none listed until modern times. There was one of these in 1899 and in 1975 two. Contemporary engineers were: auto-electrical (2); panel beater (1); civil engineering contractors (2); electrical (7); general (4); heating (6); motor (9) and structural (1).

Similarly an analysis of manufacturers is only valid in a few cases:

Activity	1822	1853	1899	1974
Brewers/maltsters	7	8	5	1
Gas	none	none	1	1
Millers	3	2	3	1
Mineral waters	none	none	2	1
Milk products	none	none	1	1
Silk	none	none	1	none

Modern (1975) records give in addition office equipment (4); builders (9); chemical (1); manufacturing chemists (1); clothing (1); contact lens (1); concrete (1); engineering (4); electrical (6); electronic (3); fasteners (4); food products (4); heat exchangers (1); measuring and other instruments (4); meat products (1); metal section (1); mining equipment (1); packaging (2); records (1); rubber products (1); steel fabricators (1); TV aerials (1); tents (1) and waterproof goods (1).

Services have by and large increased in diversity, and 1975 facilities with no traditional equivalent were beauty therapists (1); carpet cleaners (1); ceiling contractors (1); cellulose sprayers (1); cinemas (2); dry cleaners (4); electricity (1); factory cleaners (1); employment agencies (5); kennels (1); lamination consultants (1); office cleaners (2); office equipment suppliers (4); plant hire (1); plasterers (1); plastic coating services (1); property developers (5); publishers (4); tenpin bowling (1); roofing and tiling contractors (3); stove enamelling (2); turf accountants (5); window cleaners (2); woodworm control (1) and advertising, PR and Promotion heading the list inevitably with 6.

For the rest, needs have clearly changed.

Apart from the Aylesbury Market Co, listed only in 1899, and the Canal Co, listed in 1822, there were two boat owners in 1853, two canal carriers and wharfingers in 1823 and still in 1899, and an 1899 feather cleaner (!) and four livery stables in 1853.

Activity	1822	1853	1899	1974
Taxi/car hire	none	none	1	10
Chimney sweeps	none	2	5	1
Easting houses	none	2	2	24
Laundresses/laundries	none	none	13	6
Newspapers	1	3	3	2

Activity	1922	1853	1899	1974
Oil	none	none	1	2
Pawnbroker	none	none	1	none
Undertakers	none	2	?	2
Water supply	none	none	1	1
Carriers	24	47	67	18

Activity	1822	1853	1899	1974
Inns/hotels (inc. one Temperance establishment in 1899)	38	43	50	39

(There were two vintners, four innkeepers and 25 alehouse keepers—in 1577!)

The above analysis is as comprehensive as listings allowed in 1974, but is not necessarily exhaustive, especially as far as contemporary Aylesbury is concerned.

The list that follows was a cross section of current Aylesbury trade and industry in 1975, drawn solely from replies to questionnaires sent to organisations in the town. No responsibility is accepted by author or publisher for any errors of any kind.

			Established
Adams Garage Aylesbury	Tring Road	Motor trade	1928
Antiference Ltd	Bicester Road	TV and leisure products	1952
Askeys Ltd	Stocklake	Cone/wafer biscuits	1964
Aylesbury Toxophily Crafts Ltd	Walton Road	Archery equipment suppliers	1963
Bucks Herald	Exchange Street	Local weekly newspaper	1832
G. W. Curtis	Lower Friar Square	Pet/Garden store	1970
Drs B. G. Dooley, Sylvia Dooley, L. I. Holmes-Smith	Meadowcroft	Medical practitioners	1964
Fosters Taxis and Minibus Service	Cock Lane off New Street	Taxis and minibuses	1962
Foster Wiggins & Co	Church Street	Chartered Accountants	1970
The Great Western	Buckingham Street	Cafe/Restaurant	1974
Jarvis, Halliday & Co Ltd	Bicester Road	Wine shippers	1928
Klockner-Moeller Ltd	Gatehouse Close	Motor control/switchgear	
Lucas Service Overseas Ltd	Haddenham	Exporters automotive components	1958
Ron Miller Ltd	Southern Road	Dairymen	1961
The Nestle Company Ltd	High Street	Food manufacturers	1870
Pertec	Griffin Lane	Adhesive manufacturer	1960
Rediffusion Central Services Ltd	Gatehouse Road	Management Services: Rediffusion	1971
Shaw & Kilburn Ltd	Cambridge Street	Vauxhall/Bedford products	1945
West Bros	California	Upholsterers/flooring contractors	1946
Rexel Ltd	Gatehouse Road	Manufacturers of office products	1965

Note: The above analysis was researched in 1974/5 and still stands as a record and as a comparison over 150 years.

LEFT: Was someone born with a 'silver' (street) spoon
in the 17th century?

ABOVE: Somebody certainly threw this 18th century slipware bowl on the
Market Square rubbish tip.

RIGHT: Stone windmill.

ABOVE: Two more trade tokens. (County Museum)

BELOW: The Market Square c1840. (Margaret Sale)

ABOVE: Another view of Market Square. The lock-up is marked +.
(Margaret Sale)

BELOW: Sharp & Sons, coppersmiths, Walton Street—translated to York
Museum in 1958. (The cottages behind were demolished in 1920).
(Osterfield)

ABOVE: The 1808 Market House, demolished 1866.

BELOW: The Corn Exchange (Town Hall Arches) erected 1865.

AYLESBURY
MARKET COMPANY SHARES.

GADSDEN AND SON

WILL SELL BY AUCTION,

At the GEORGE HOTEL, AYLESBURY,

On Wednesday, 22nd December, 1869,

At Four for Five o'Clock to a Minute,

TEN
£10 SHARES

IN THE

AYLESBURY MARKET COMPANY
ALL PAID UP.

Further Particulars of Messrs. PARROTT, Aylesbury, or of the AUCTIONEERS.

Printed at the "Bucks Herald" Steam Printing Offices, Kingsbury, Aylesbury.

ABOVE: The Market Square after 1865. (Ralph May)

BELOW: 1869 Market Co share sale. (Osterfield)

ABOVE: On the back of this 1864 share certificate for the Market Co is a
note of the liquidation return—£2 0s 3⅜d in 1902. (Hayward Parrott)

BELOW: Lounging in the Square, before the clock
went up in 1876. (Osterfield)

94

ABOVE: Market Day. (County Record Office)

BELOW: Pillow lace makers from Waddesdon. (Osterfield)

ABOVE: Silk shuttles and the product itself from Aylesbury silk mill. (County Museum)

LEFT: An Aylesbury plaiter's straw splitter. (Margaret Sale)

RIGHT: One of Stone's clocks. (County Museum)

BELOW: The osier beds. (Margaret Sale)

ABOVE: Kingham's stores in the 19th century.

BELOW: A concourse of carts in Kingsbury Square. (Both Margaret Sale)

ABOVE: The famous ducks on Walton pond, c1900. (Hayward Parrott)

BELOW: Local transaction, 1878. (Osterfield)

LEFT: The late William 'Ducky' Weston of Mount Street—last of the family to breed Aylesbury ducks commercially, in 1956. (Hayward Parrott)

RIGHT: North and Randall's mineral waters in a 19th century Codd bottle. (Ralph May)

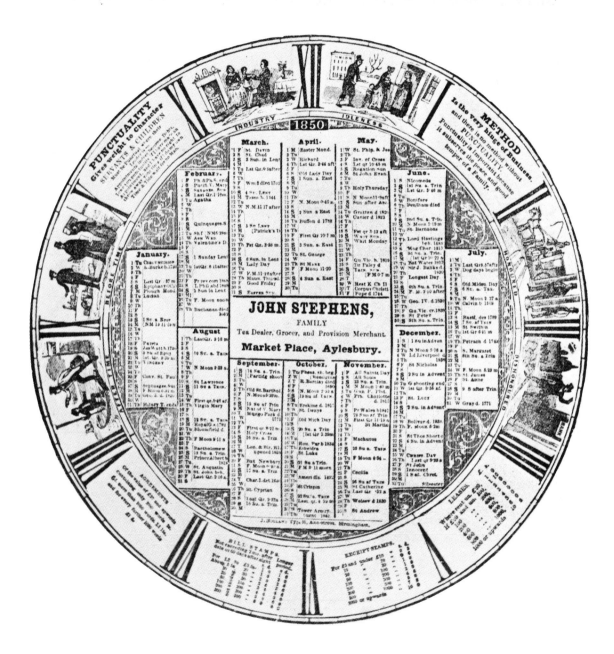

ABOVE: The masthead for the 1836 Aylesbury News.

BELOW: Advertising circular in 1850. (Margaret Sale)

ABOVE: 1898 Bucks Herald staff. (Margaret Sale)

BELOW: Hanging, swinging billhead of 1871. (Hayward Parrott)

ABOVE: Mr Ivatts and his shoe shop.

BELOW: Bring us yer washing! (Both Margaret Sale)

ABOVE : The brewery. (Bucks Reference Library)

LEFT : Locke's Hartwell Road brickworks.

RIGHT : The product in 1836. (Both Ralph May)

ABOVE LEFT: Three 1867 advertisements. (Osterfield)

BELOW CENTRE AND LEFT: Town and country shops at the turn of the
century—Ing's of Haddenham and Smith's of Market Street. (Osterfield
and Hayward Parrott)

ABOVE RIGHT: Anglo-Swiss Condensed Milk Co, delivering the goods
from High Street in 1873.

RIGHT: Hunt Barnard took over this 1889 bakery from Mr Wheeler in
1898, leaving for Milton Street in 1927. (Both Osterfield)

1. Works and Luncheon Tent.   2. The Exhibition.   3. Decorating Prize Winners.   4. Effluent Water.   5. Exterior Exhibition Tent.   6. Produce grown with Native Guano Manure.

SKETCHES AT THE NATIVE GUANO COMPANY'S ANNUAL SHOW AT AYLESBURY.

The Native Guano Co's annual show in 1882.

ABOVE: Hazell, Watson & Viney's Tring Road factory shortly after it was
built. (Bucks Reference Library)

BELOW: The early Iris and the 1970's Llama.

ABOVE: Cruikshank captures the local hare hunters. (County Museum)

BELOW: The Aylesbury steeplechase in full flight and fall.
(Margaret Sale)

Time Off

Aylesbury's famous steeplechase sums up the town's past: horse and field for transport and farming; Fleet Marston in the background of Turner's print (reproduced on the cover) neatly underlining this with a reminder of the first major road junction. In fact, the 'chase was not under way until 1836—the date of Turner's prints. But flat racing was a regular attraction at Aylesbury as long ago as 1684. Quainton Meadow was the site for Dukes and commoners to assemble for the racing—and the gambling. Then in 1754 Haydon Hill took over, and finally the event moved to Weedon field until its disappearance in 1815.

The races were always run in August, brought many visitors, gave the excuse for a ball in the town, and brought substantial custom to the inns and taverns, which also offered a side-attraction: 'cocking as usual'.

Aylesbury's taverns and inns grew in number and splendour with the growth of travel. But as far back as 1577, the town boasted two 'vinteners', four innholders and twenty-five 'aylehowsekepers'; the whole of Bucks contained but five vintners, 92 innholders and 325 alehouse keepers, so Aylesbury was at the top of the league table.

By the 19th century the number of beershops, inns, hotels and taverns had grown to thirty-eight, and in 1899 the total reached seventy-nine!

That same year there was a single temperance hotel to strike a balance. Arguably the most famous of Aylesbury's inns is the old King's Head—dating back to 1450 but now largely 17th century in structure, it originally consisted of four ranges of buildings round a court-yard, including a hall of five bays since reduced to two. Original glass shows the arms of Henry VI and Margaret of Anjou his wife.

In 1823 beer was given away in the Market Place 'to allcomers' to celebrate the birth of Earl Temple. But certainly the most convivial of Aylesbury's drinking houses in the past was the White Hart. In 1815 they handled the matter of eating magnificently at the White Hart. There follows a Bill of fare:

First Course: Turtle Soup, Potatoes, Lobster Sauce, Melted Butter, Turbot.

Second Course: Boiled Fowls, Harricot Mutton, Oyster Sauce, Beef Olives, Tongue, Turnips and Carrots, Mint Sauce, Greens, Saddle of Lamb, Stewed Pigeons, Salad, Veal Olives, Boiled Leg of Pork, French Beans, Potatoes, Pease Pudding, Cauliflower, Tremlong of Beef, Roast Fowls.

Third Course: Sweet Sauce, Brace of Birds, Bread Sauce, Potatoes, Hare.

Fourth Course: Jelly, Gooseberry Pie, Blancmange, Custards, Baked Apple Pudding, Apricot Tart, Plum Pie, Blancmange, Boiled Plum Pudding, Fruit in Jelly, and Port, Sherry, Claret, Champagne and Turtle Punch.

The bill came to one pound ten shillings a head—with wine. The food was laid course by course and carved and served from the table—not by waiters. At one such repast, Squire

Drake of Amersham gave seventy gentlemen a meal which included a single course of twenty-six dishes of fish.

Good Cheer, good Humor, and good Neighbourhood were the sole aims of the Aylesbury Club, formed in 1810 to meet on the Friday nearest the full moon in each month from November to April, and including among its membership Earl Temple, Lord George Grenville, the Rev Sir George Lee, Bart, Col Nugent and other well-known townsmen. The subscription was two guineas a year for wine, with 7s 6d for dinner. Dinner was to be served 'precisely' at four o'clock, and the wine restricted to one bottle for each person present. 'Such Members as choose to remain after the President has quitted the Chair, to pay for the Wine they may call for, at the rate of six shillings per bottle.'

Sometimes the eating got out of hand: on January 21, 1832 an inquest found that Robert Brazil died by choking on stewed beef at Judkins' bakehouse, where he had been 'eating voraciously.'

Gargantuan appetites were not abnormal: a man named Foster of Quainton on March 2, 1821 ate '6 lbs of bacon, a peck of potatoes, and a Quartern loaf, and drank a gallon of ale in three hours; he would undertake to swallow Quainton windmill if they would give him time.'

Pigeon pie profited but poorly when in 1821 (February) a shooting match was held between six Aylesburians and six villagers at the Horse and Jockey. Thirty-six birds were loosed—thirty-four survived. Only one man scored, and he hit both the unlucky ones. The match was an annual affair.

This was the sumptuous side to life in the county capital and market town. But the 'cocking as usual' that dominated the race broadsheets represented the seamier side. The cock-fight was the main attraction once the races were over and the gentry had repaired to the White Hart and elsewhere. The Aylesbury cockpit was upstairs in the old Market House.

Some of the gentry attended the cockpit and large sums were won and lost on this or that bird. The 'sport' was not confined to race week, and reached an annual peak on Shrove Tuesday, and at Hartwell Show and Bierton Feast. Often the result caused bloodshed among the onlookers as well as the birds; at the Two Brewers in Buckingham Street in 1840 one cock owner had his arm broken, following a disputed victory.

Hale Leys, once a field, was the popular site of another pastime involving the fighting cocks—cock throwing, where clubs were thrown at the birds, which when felled, had to be overtaken by the thrower to claim victory, bird and the right to charge others to try their arm. Another popular site was the Churchyard Avenue. Cock-throwing survived longer at Quainton than in the town—at least until 1844.

Rock concerts at Friars seem tame by comparison to Aylesbury's past pursuits, and chief among these was badger baiting—the old Market House boasted a badger-hole for the purpose. The pastime had disappeared by the 1820's. By contrast dog-fighting was commonly promoted in the streets of the town, and long after Aylesbury had lost interest, local villagers continued the sport, the parish constable at Brill setting up a match for £50 in 1843—and charging half a crown to spectators. From Elizabethan times, bull baiting was a popular way to pass some part of the time on the days when fairs were held. Kingsbury, Market Square, Temple Square and Market Hill were the usual sites, and in 1820 the inhabitants celebrated by collecting the money to buy a bull for baiting in front of County Hall.

If racing was the sport of kings and cocking the prerogative of the gentry, bull-baiting was the people's sport. One bull baiting at Stocklake featured a prisoner's bull-dog borrowed by the Gaoler. The affair reached the courts and the magistrate, Col Brown told him: 'It's of no use to send you to prison, Sheriff, because you are there already; you must be fined.' 1821 saw the last bull-baiting in Aylesbury, when the promoters were indicted for riot. Constable William Cross had told one Slaughter (aptly named), William Adams and Robert Bonnick that they could not proceed in the town. The three men tied the bull to the Kingsbury pump rail and let the dogs loose, then released it, letting it run down the street, still roped, with some 150 people following. The whole concourse swept round the Market Place, into Walton Street, and back past the Oxford Arms and Bulls Head. Shops were shut in a hurry and the majority barricaded themselves in for fear of their lives. The promoters were fined 1s, imprisoned for a week and bound over, but it was allowed they had not realised their actions were illegal.

Surprisingly in view of the emphasis on duck-rearing for the London trade, setting dogs to duck-hunting was another popular local sport, and one which survived long after 'cocking' had ceased. It was a favourite Sunday morning diversion, usually out of town on a quiet reach of the canal. The pits and ponds near Cambridge Street were probably another favourite haunt of the duck-hunters; hence the Dog and Duck public house.

Aylesbury's sporting instinct was not confined to the abuse of animals and birds; the nationally popular spectator sport of pugilism, forerunner to today's boxing tournaments, was a highlight of fair and market. In May 1823 Young Dolly Eldridge fought Jack Slaughter, at Hulcot Trunk, to evade the constables. They were Aylesbury men. Dolly was Bucks champion, but he lost then, and again in November to Bromley the gardener, at the New Inn. He got his revenge against Bromley in 1825. Bonnick the bull baiter seconded.

Gentler sports were played, when the Aylesbury squadron of the Bucks Yeomanry played cricket that same summer; 50 guineas was the prize and the sides were drawn from married and single men respectively. But Aylesbury's cricketers lost at home and away to Leighton, in the club's first season. They triumphed over Wycombe but lost to Risborough in 1823, and trounced Leighton two years later.

Art was not entirely ignored, and the Committee of the Aylesbury Amateur Concerts, meeting in 1823 were treated to 'several songs' by Lord Nugent, while Mr Rickford 'would but he couldn't.' On the other hand, Mr Hyriott's concert in May had a 'poor attendance, and he will lose by it.' The Amateur Society's concert suffered similarly, though the Misses Hyriott 'maintained their reputation' for duets. Organist Hyriott died in April 1824 aged 49 and the last concert was held the same month. On December 1, 1823 Mr Jackman's theatre was opened and enjoyed full houses almost immediately. In 1827 he met with poor attendance. That week also saw the tenth anniversary of the Aylesbury Book Club, and in 1821 a lending library was launched to supply the poor with 'suitable books free.' Today the County Library incorporates the Lending and Reference Libraries and the Buckingham Collection.

Aylesbury United FC was founded in 1897; the town RFC in 1932.

In 1826 the big barn behind the church was converted for Jackman's theatre. A different kind of theatrical event never got off the ground when one Courtney, who had walked forty miles backward on a quarter mile stretch of local ground, sought permission to 'fly' across the town by means of a rope tied to the steeple of St Mary's. The Rev Morley told him he could not encourage a man to fly away from the church, but if he liked to fly up to the weathercock he would not interfere. Courtney 'thinking this an uphill job, declined.'

Courtney was not the only high flyer. Mr Green was much occupied with his balloon, which experienced a series of accidents over the years, until in 1848 'an immense crowd' watched a successful ascent from Hinds Field in Bierton, and a 'soft' landing near Cheddington Station.

Hunting was a favourite pursuit, and while Baron Rothschild's hounds rampaged up and down the town's thoroughfares, toppling those who got in the way in 1842, that same year the Long Crendon Sparrow Club proudly announced their bag of 271,831 sparrows.

The Baron's hounds were not the only ones; the Royal Staghounds met in the Vale, often after the steeplechases, and these perhaps were Aylesbury's most popular and spectacular events. In February 1836 the combination of staghounds and steeplechase gave the town a 'gay week.'

The Aylesbury 'chase started in 1836, when purses rarely exceeded £50 with perhaps a 20 sovereign sweepstake. The 1836 event became an annual gathering, with a fund raised to compensate farmers, which after a while failed to pay. The races ceased for a few years, then revived, when a dispute at Banbury brought the undergraduate contest between Oxford students to Aylesbury.

1846 saw the new 'chases inaugurated, at Broughton. Eventually the Grand National Hunt Steeplechase came to the Long Meadow, and the inter-varsity races were held there too, the undergraduates riding under aliases to avoid identification and disapproval by the university authorities, in what became known as the Aylesbury Aristocratic Steeplechases.

In those races, rarely more than six mounts out of some 15 survived the course. In 1853 one race ran a dead heat and was re-run for a mere £7 stake. The course finally moved to the Prebendal Farm estate, where it was still located in 1894. In 1874 the Grand National Hunt meeting attracted a £1,200 gate and the stewards included the Prince of Wales, Disraeli and several lords and knights of the realm. The last meeting was held in 1929.

Matters of history have long been recorded by the Architectural and Archaeological Society for the County of Buckingham, founded November 16, 1847, who in more modern guise maintain a muniments room at the County Museum, itself founded in that year. The Museum moved in 1908 and extended into Ceely House in 1944. Today the Literary

The County Theatre, sadly no more, was originally the old Market Theatre, founded by the Aylesbury Electric Theatre Co in 1911, as a music hall. Destroyed by fire in 1924 it was rebuilt that year, closed for the duration of the last war and reopened at the New Market Theatre in 1947. The Grand Pavilion opened 1925, was enlarged in 1936 and became the Granada in 1947. It was joined by the Odeon, in 1937.

But perhaps the most famous incident in Aylesbury's repertoire of fun and games followed the earlier feat of the Marquis of Waterford in taking a horse upstairs at the White Hart, feeding him from the table, and taking him down again. In 1851, table talk during the 'chase stewards' dinner in the Rochester Room turned to this feat. It was suggested that 'the little grey' would repeat the achievement, and he was duly brought up.

The horse was then led to jump two chairs, when J. Leech Manning, a sporting farmer undertook to jump the table mounted on the grey. The room was forty feet long, and Manning mounted bare back, took the grey to one corner, and then with a slap, jumped the table, food, wine and candles and all, turned, and jumped it again. Another rider, a parson, repeated the feat—both ways—and the horse was led away, but refused the stairs. Eventually blindfolded, he made the descent, and years after was shown off by his later owner as 'the gallant grey that had jumped the table at the Rochester Room at Aylesbury.'

WHITE HART HOTEL,
AYLESBURY.

CATALOGUE OF THE IMPORTANT & UNRESERVED SALE
OF EXCELLENT

HOUSEHOLD FURNITURE,
SITTING & DINING ROOM SUITES,
WELL-APPOINTED BEDROOMS, CAPITAL KITCHEN REQUISITES,
CABINET PIANOFORTE, RICHLY-CUT GLASS,
PLATE AND PLATED ARTICLES, LINEN, CHINA,
CIGARS, BOOKS, ENGRAVINGS,
CARRIAGES, HORSES, HARNESS,
Valuable and Extensive FIXTURES, Capital GREENHOUSE, Bedding-out and other PLANTS, and various other EFFECTS,

Which will be Sold by Auction, by

MR. T. FOWLER,

On **WEDNESDAY, THURSDAY, and FRIDAY, MARCH** 30th and 31st and **APRIL 1st, 1864,**

By order of Mr. J. K. FOWLER, in consequence of his having sold the Hotel and Premises to The Aylesbury Market Company.

SALE TO COMMENCE EACH DAY AT ELEVEN O'CLOCK PUNCTUALLY.

ORDER OF SALE:

FIRST DAY.—Linen, Cutlery, Cigars, and a portion of Sitting and Bed Room Furniture.

SECOND DAY.—Silver and Plated Goods, Glass and China, Books and Engravings, with some of the principal Sitting and Bed Room Furniture, together with the Laundry Fixtures.

THIRD DAY.—House and Trade Fixtures, Carriages, Harness, and Horses, together with the Greenhouse, Bedding-out and other Plants, and out-door miscellaneous Property and Effects.

Catalogues obtainable at the Place of Sale; BUCKS HERALD Office, Aylesbury; of the AUCTIONEER, 86, High-street, Banbury; and Mr. METCALFE, 41, Poultry, London.

The Whole may be Viewed on Tuesday, March 29th, and the Mornings of Sale

PRINTED AT THE BUCKS HERALD STEAM PRINTING OFFICES, AYLESBURY.

ABOVE LEFT: End of the White Hart in 1864. (Bucks Reference Library)

ABOVE RIGHT: The last view of this famous coaching house.

CENTRE: White Hart heyday—a mid-19th century billhead. (Both Hayward Parrott)

BELOW: The Bell, Market Square, early this century. (Osterfield)

ABOVE RIGHT: 1851 billhead for the Bull's Head, demolished 1970.
(Hayward Parrott)

ABOVE LEFT: The old Borough Arms, Park Street and Cambridge Street,
demolished 1960. (E. D. Hollowday)

BELOW LEFT: The George Inn, now no more. (Hayward Parrott)

BELOW RIGHT: Teetotal tearooms. (Margaret Sale)

Grand Volunteer
RIFLE 🏵 FÊTE,
AT VELVET LAWN,
On MONDAY, 13th of AUG., 1860.

Presentation of a Silver Bugle and Colors
TO THE
4th BUCKS RIFLE VOLUNTEERS.

A Muster of the Vale of Aylesbury, 4th Bucks, will take place on the above-named day, in the beautiful Grounds of Velvet Lawn, kindly granted for the occasion by Lady Frankland Russell.

Detachments from other Corps are expected to be present.

THE SPLENDID

Band of the 1st Life Guards

Under the direction of Mr. Waddell, will attend during the day, and perform their choicest Music.

LOCAL BANDS ARE ALSO ENGAGED.

The Vale of Aylesbury (4th Bucks) Corps, headed by their Drum and Fife Band, will March on the Ground at 2 p.m. under the Command of Captain the Hon. F. G. H. IRBY.

The Presentation of the Silver Bugle (by Lady Frankland Russell), and a Color (by the Hon. Mrs. Caulfield Pratt), will take place at 2.30 p.m. precisely; after which

THE EVOLUTIONS OF THE RIFLE VOLUNTEERS

Will commence, under the Command of Lieutenant-Colonel Caulfield Pratt.

RUSTIC GAMES AND VARIOUS AMUSEMENTS
WILL THEN BE ORGANISED.   BALLOON ASCENTS.

THE ORDINARY

Will take place, under a spacious Marquee, punctually at 4 o'Clock. The Band of the Life Guards will perform during the Repast. Every accommodation will be afforded for the comfort of those Ladies who may honor the Dinner with their presence.

AN AL FRESCO BALL

Will take place to the Quadrille Music of the Life Guards. Accommodation will be provided for Horses, &c. at a fixed charge.

☞ Every Person found on the Grounds without a proper Ticket will be required to leave, and Persons must produce their Tickets when desired by any of the Committee.

The Committee request that both Dinner and Admission Tickets may be taken on or before Wednesday, August 8th, as the regulation as to increased Charges after that date will be strictly adhered to.

TICKETS for Dinner and Admission to the Grounds may be had of Mr S Gibbs, Mr G C Bennett, Mr. J. K. Fowler, Mr. Lehmann, and Mr. J. Verney, Aylesbury.

DE FRAINE AND SON, PRINTERS, *BUCKS CHRONICLE AND BUCKS GAZETTE* PRINTING OFFICES, WALTON STREET, AYLESBURY.

Army antics to amuse Aylesburians in 1860. (Margaret Sale)

THEATRE, AYLESBURY.

By Desire, of the Members, of

The Benefit Society,

Held at the COCK INN, and the

Macbeth, Mr. COULDOCK, Duncan, King at ... HAMBLETON.
Malcolm, Mr. HARTLEY, Banquo, Mr. JACKMAN.
Macduff, Mr. H. FENTON, Rosse, Mr. C. JACKMAN,
Donalbain, Mr. PARTLETON, Fleance, Miss L. JACKMAN,
Lady Macbeth, Mrs. HARTLEY, Waiting Lady, Mrs. PARTLETON,

WITCHES.

Hecate, Mr. HARTLEY, 1s. Witch, Mrs. H. FENTON.
2nd, Witch, Miss S. JACKMAN, 3rd Witch, Mrs. JACKMAN,

After which the Musical PIECE, of

Quarter Day

Or, A New Way to Pay your Rent.

Sir Amorous Grey, Mr. HAMBLETON, Gripeall, his Steward, Mr. HARTLEY,
Crispin, A Cobler, Mr. JACKMAN,
Lady Grey, Mrs. JACKMAN, Maud, the Cobler's Wife, Mrs. H. FENTON.

A COMIC SONG, by Mr. HAMBLETON.
A FAVOURITE SONG, by Mrs. H. Fenton,
And A COMIC SONG, by Mr. HARTLEY.

To conclude with the Popular Musical FARCE, of THE

Illustrious Stranger,

Or, MARRIED and BURIED.

Abdallar, King of the Island, Mr. COULDOCK, Prince Assp, Mr. HARTLEY,
Benjamin Bowbell, ... Officer, Mr. JACKMAN, Gimino, Mr. H. FENTON, Zinquo, Mr. HAMBLETON,
Mr. C. JACKMAN, Guard, Mr. PARTLETON,
Princess Ixe, Miss S. JACKMAN, Fatima, Mrs. H. FENTON, Leiwe, &c.&c.

Nights of Playing Monday, Wednesday, Thursday, Friday, & Saturday.
All Demands on the Theatre, are requested to be sent in immediately,
as the Theatre Finally Closes ON SATURDAY NEXT.

BOXES 2s. 6d. half price 1s. 6d.—— PIT 7s. 6d. half price 1s.
GALLERY 1s. half price 6d.——HALF-PRICE at half past Eight.
Tickets may be had of Mr. & Mrs. Hartley, at the Crown Inn & of Mr. May.
Doors open at half past SIX and begin at SEVEN o'Clock precisely.

Aylesbury Market Theatre

Proprietors: The Aylesbury Electric Theatre, Limited.
Manager: M. BROOKS. Telephone: 68, Aylesbury.

Varieties & Pictures

Two Performances Nightly, at 6-30 and 8-30

Matinee: Saturday at 2-30.

Acknowledged by all to show the — Finest, Clearest and Best Animated Pictures.
MIRTH! MYSTERY! COMEDY! DRAMA!
Latest Topicals in Pathe's Weekly Animated Gazette.

Entire Change of Programme Monday & Thursday.

Popular Prices: 3d., 6d., 9d., & 1/= Children 2d.
9d. and 1s. Seats (Reserved and Numbered) can be booked without extra charge.

See Bills for Full Programme.

ABOVE: Mr Jackman's players at your pleasure.
(Bucks Reference Library)

BELOW: Animated wonders of the kinematographic age. (Osterfield)

ABOVE: Aylesbury on the ball in the early days. (F. J. Cromack)

BELOW: Leech Manning takes the grey over the table at the White Hart's
Rochester Room in 1851. (County Museum)

AYLES BURY

1778

44 AYLES BURY

1790

AYLESBURY

1795

AYLESBURY 48

1804

AYLESBURY 42

1828

AYLESBURY
AU 29
1832

THE FIRST DATED MARK

AYLSBURY
SP 28
1842
†

Aylesbury Py Post

1835

A LOCAL PENNY POST BETWEEN
AYLESBURY AND WADDESDON

AYLESBURY
AP 13
1849
3

AYLESBURY
OC 8
1855
B

AYLESBURY
JAI 5
58

ABOVE: The Birmingham Mail snowbound in 1836. (Osterfield)

BELOW: Aylesbury postmarks. (The numbers give the mileage from London.) (Hayward Parrott)

By the Way

If early man trod tracks along the ridge of the Chilterns, it was because this route was easiest cleared. The Icknield Way skirted Aylesbury's future site. The first indication of Aylesbury's future significance as a junction was the driving of the Roman Watling Street to the north, crossing the Icknield Way at Dunstable not far off.

With Verulamium (St Albans) growing in importance as a Roman centre, Akeman Street was engineered to take the military and trade from Verulamium, by way of Tring and Aston Clinton to Fleet Marston en route for Alcester. Another road drives north-west from Fleet Marston—the beginning of the network of routes that were to crystallise in Aylesbury's development as a centre for trade and county administration.

The line of Akeman Street dips southwards now to pass through the town, but a glance at a modern map shows how once it bypassed it, and the remnant of the subsidiary route can be seen running through Berryfield to pass Quainton to the north east.

Today the radial system approaches the town from Tring, Wendover, Kimble, Stone, Waddesdon, Whitchurch and Wing—all main roads.

The Roman roads were firmly founded; the other routes were little more than tracks.

But the Roman junction and the choice of Aylesbury's drier, higher site for settlement focussed the infant system on the town. The nature of the relatively marshy ground could well have inhibited their development, but successive lords of the manors in and around Aylesbury bequeathed funds and built causeways, and gradually the system grew. In 1457 Edmund Brudenell, Lord of Stoke Mandeville, left £40 to sort out the Stoke Mandeville-Aylesbury road. Thirty-three years later Sir Ralph Verney left ten pounds for 'the reparacione and amendying of noyous and ruynous weyes nere about Aylesbury and Flete Marston' and William Hampden of Hartwell also contributed. In 1493 John Bedford made funds available for 'the perpetual amendment of the highways in and about Aylesbury' while a three-mile causeway was constructed from Aylesbury towards London, known as the Hartwell Causeway.

By this time the town was an important market centre, and by the 17th century it gained significance as a garrison. Roads tend to gain where the military have a need for efficient movement of men and goods, and by that time Aylesbury was astride the main route not only to the north of the county and the old capital, Buckingham, and a central point for politicians, landowners and agricultural trade, but was a principal gateway to the Midlands.

It was inevitable that it should become a coaching centre. The London-Birmingham mailcoach paused at Aylesbury; so did the London-Banbury route—particularly significant as the latter town grew in importance as a cattle mart, paralleling Aylesbury's significance in the same business. The Birmingham route ran up from Amersham and Wendover, and thence through the town to Buckingham and beyond; the London travellers had a choice

119

too, along the coach route through Watford, Tring and then Aylesbury. The original junction was in fact at Walton, and the roads were common through the town itself. The two great university towns of Oxford and Cambridge made connection through Thame, Aylesbury and Bierton. In 1795 a turnpike was planned from Wycombe to the town. And in 1826 'New Road' was laid, now the High Street, and this brought the Tring road right into the town centre, though now the old road pattern has reasserted itself with the construction of the one way system.

Five years before that, there had been serious disagreement on the line of the new road, and it was not settled until 1825, when Sparrow's Herne Turnpike Trust met, decided and planned demolition of houses between the George and the Crown. The road cost £7,000. When Aylesburians were arguing about New Road, turnpike charges between Aylesbury and Bicester were doubled to 4s 6d for Sunday traffic: 'They don't mind you breaking the Sabbath if you pay double'. Turnpike troubles mounted with objections in 1823 to the location of the gates, and that year it was decided to lower Tring Road by 36 ft and put the ballast in the valley to improve the road there. The Bicester turnpike was further improved in 1825, and the Aylesbury and Hockliffe Turnpike Trustees lowered their charges that same year—the year when the keeper at Padbury Gate was bound, gagged and robbed.

Nonetheless, the roads were still in a bad state in the early 19th century, largely due to their tendency to flood or turn into quagmires. In 1790, the Warwick mail hit the guard rails at Bell Corner, and pitched the guard into a pig-sty!

The Aylesbury coach can be dated back certainly to 1662, and there is evidence that a coach plied through the town in 1712, but the Act promoting the Bicester-Aylesbury turnpike was passed in 1770 and in 1795 the first stage coach ran the route. In 1820 there was a service from Reading, and that year the 'Old Aylesbury Coach' made local history driving to London and back within the day. Dale and Tollett promoted it and Thomas Wootton was coachman. But it was James Wyatt and the Aylesbury Dispatch which made Aylesbury's coaching reputation, and presumably proprietor Joseph Hearn's fortune. Before the railways took over, more than twelve coaches thundered through the town daily.

But before the roads improved and the coaches became more reliable, the waggoners provided transport, and in 1726 Robert King drove the Bicester waggon, advising highwayman friend Drury whenever he anticipated worthwhile loot aboard. Hijacking trucks is no new phenomenon. In 1755 the Warwick stage was robbed this side of Wendover and relieved of £10. In 1784 Joseph Radley was one of several highwaymen executed at Aylesbury. He kept accounts of his profits, among which are numbered 'Earl of Buckinghamshire . . . £36 15s 6d'. The total came to £308 8s 0d. Another to meet his end on the Aylesbury gallows was 'Galloping Dick' Richard Ferguson—in 1800.

Pigot's directory lists eight coach services in 1822: to London, Banbury, Bicester and Beddington, Birmingham, Cambridge, Kidderminster, Oxford, and to Winslow. The London coaches were the Royal Mail arriving at two in the morning, the Regulator, the Despatch, the Union and 'a Coach'. In addition carriers were providing local services, and Joseph Hearn's offered a London service daily 'Mondays and Thursdays excepted'.

In January 1836 two coach proprietors found themselves in direct conflict, with Hearn's 'Wonder' competing with Bayntum's 'No Wonder' on the London route. Hearn, with coachman Wyatt up, charged 12s inside and 7s outside for the trip, and Wyatt made the journey in 3 hours and 35 minutes. That same year a snowstorm halted virtually all traffic, the mail losing 24 hours, and the Birmingham coach taking 20 hours to make 38 miles.

In 1853 Oxford was listed by carriers as the only long distance facility by road—the canal and railways had taken over. Carriers' carts in 1899 were exclusively local.

The canals brought the first simple means of bulk transport of heavy goods, and in 1790 the Oxford Canal was completed, passing within 25 miles of the town. Nine years later the Wendover branch of the Grand Junction opened to traffic, but five miles away. It took another fifteen years for Aylesbury to obtain its own branch, which opened in 1814.

In 1835 Aylesbury's leaders saw the possibilities—and the threats—of the steam railway, legislated for by Parliament in 1801. While other towns fought the new-fangled locomotion, Aylesbury laid its plans. Stephenson's inter-city London to Birmingham railway opened three years later and in 1839, it had given birth—to the Aylesbury branch.

Stephenson stated the proposed track was the easiest with which he had ever contended. Meanwhile coaches were plying to Tring Station, when one was upset and the coachman hurt, the year before Aylesbury obtained its own rail link. The journey to London on the new track took two hours ten minutes and cost 5s 6d. There were 1,199 passengers in the first month, and goods traffic reduced on the canal as the railway gathered momentum.

With the railway a patent success, coachman Wyatt retired, to universal testimonials.

But in 1845 the now familiar complaints of poor service centred on delays in journey time—now three hours to town. Rail accidents were commonplace, though there were no major accidents until the major disaster of 1904 at the Station when three were killed and four injured, as the London train was derailed, and a parcel train ran into it.

In 1863 the Great Western Railway was connected to the town from Princes Risborough, and in 1868 connection was made with Oxford with the construction of the Aylesbury and Buckingham railway via Verney Junction—originally planned in 1846!

In 1823 the postal service (started in 1685) was daily, by mail cart for distances, and foot-post locally. By 1853 the London mail had achieved twice daily frequency. By 1899 there were seven and more collections—from sub post offices alone.

In 1892 the Metropolitan Railway reached out direct from London to Aylesbury, and in 1899 the Great Central from the Midlands used those same tracks to thunder straight through to Marylebone Station.

Strangely, Stephenson originally planned his London and North Western Railway from London through Uxbridge and Amersham to Aylesbury, but landowner opposition was so extensive that Countess Bridgewater suggested he follow the line of the Grand Junction Canal across her land at Berkhamsted and Tring where the land had already been gashed for the waterway; there was no opposition to this, and so that particular line missed the town and became the Euston Inter-City route we know today.

The railways cut distance as never before. The 1839 train cut the journey time to London from six hours to 95 minutes—at a cost of £60,000.

Today the motorways have supplanted the old coaching routes, and the canal is a backwater. Aylesbury has its own Canal Society, and in 1974 the basin of the Grand Union at Aylesbury saw 50 narrow boats moored there at an Easter rally of the Narrow Boat Owners' Association.

Bus services started at the turn of the century, and horse drawn services connected Aylesbury with Aston Clinton, Stone and Whitchurch, E. W. Young gave the town its first motorbus — to Wendover, after 1919. His Aylesbury Bus Co was taken over by the Eastern National in 1933. Then Aylesbury was served by the National Bus Co, and its own Red Rover service. Kingsbury had a bus station in 1929; the Buckingham Street Station was opened in 1949.

STAMP OFFICE
EXCHANGE TICKET
for a Day or Days under 28
County of *Buckingham*
Aylesbury Gate
RECEIVED TICKET DATED
The day of 1832
for HORSE for Day
Let from the day of 183
By of
Hired by of
(If so hired) To go to
& back, being Miles

A General Statement of the INCOME and EXPENDITURE of the BICESTER and AYLESBURY TURNPIKE TRUST, in the Counties of OXFORD and BUCKINGHAM, between the FIRST day of JANUARY and the THIRTY-FIRST day of DECEMBER, 1862.

	£ s. d.		£ s. d.
By Balance in the Treasurer's hands	11 4 11½	Balance due from the Treasurer	76 8 11½
By Allowance for Parishes reserved	0 0 0	Materials for Repairs and Cartage	255 18 10
Revenue received from Tolls	728 4 0	Manual Labour	110 0 0
Contributions received from Parishes	112 4 0	Allowances made to Parishes repairing their own Roads	83 0 0
Estimated value of Statute duty performed	0 0 0	Land Purchased	0 0 0
Revenue from Fines	0 0 0	Damage done in obtaining Materials	0 0 0
Miscellaneous Receipts	0 10 3	Tradesmen's Bills	65 0 7
Repairs of County Bridges	9 0 0	Salaries, viz:—	
Incidentals retained for Costs	0 0 0	£ s. d.	
Amount of Money borrowed on Security of Tolls	0 0 0	Treasurer ... 20 0 0	
Interest of Exchequer Bills	0 0 0	Clerk ... 25 0 0 / 85 0 0	
Balance due to the Treasurer	0 0 0	Surveyor ... 40 0 0	
		Law Charges	0 0 0
		Interest of Debt	165 0 0
		Improvements	0 0 0
		Incidental Expenses	17 7 0
		Property Tax on Interest	6 3 9½
£	**863 19 2½**	**£**	**863 19 2½**

Debts.	Rate of Interest per Cent.	Arrears of Income.	Name and Place of Abode of the Treasurer, Clerk, General and Superintending Surveyor.
Bonded Debt ... £3,300 0 0	£5	Arrears of Tolls for the current year	Joseph Parrott ... Treasurer
Unpaid Interest, to Midsummer, 1862.. 5,280 0 0		Arrears of Parish Composition for debt..	James James ... Clerk
		Arrears of other Receipts	Richard Henry Simons ... Surveyor
		Arrears of former years ... £65 : 3 : 3	All residing at Aylesbury, in the County of Buckingham.

Examined, Audited, and Allowed, at the General Annual Meeting, held at the Crooked Billet, at Ham Green, in the Hamlet of Woodham, in the County of Buckingham, this 23rd day of March, 1863.

RICHARD ROSE,
Chairman.

ABOVE LEFT: 1832 Exchange ticket for the Wendover-Buckingham turnpike at Aylesbury gate. (Hayward Parrott)

ABOVE RIGHT: White Hill—now a dual carriageway and roundabout. (Ralph May)

BELOW: Turnpike takings, 1862. (Osterfield)

C A P. XXIV.

An Act for making certain Navigable Cuts from the Towns of *Buckingham*, *Aylesbury*, and *Wendover*, in the County of *Buckingham*, to communicate with the Grand Junction Navigation, authorized to be made by an Act of the last Session of Parliament; and for amending the said Act.

[28th *March* 1794.]

HEREAS an Act was passed in the last Session of Parliament, *for making and maintaining a Navigable Canal, from the Oxford Canal Navigation at* Braunston, *in the County of* Northampton, *to join the River* Thames, *at or near* Brentford, *in the County of* Middlesex, *and also certain Collateral Cuts from the said intended Canal*; and

Preamb'e re c t s Act 33 Geo. III.

ABOVE: The canal comes in 1794. (County Record Office)

CENTRE: The canal at Walton Mill.

BELOW: LNWR station built 1839 until the new 1889 station was built.

CHEAP STEAM EXCURSION.

To London, & Back to Aylesbury

FOR 6s. 2d.

On MONDAY, the 24th Day of JULY, 1843,

A SPECIAL TRAIN

WILL leave Aylesbury Station, for London, at SIX o'Clock in the Morning. and leave Euston-Square, to return home, at HALF-PAST NINE in the Evening.

Steam boats leave London Bridge for Gravesend every half hour.

Tickets, 6s. 2d. each, for the Special Train to London and back, may be had of Mr. Muddiman, and Mr. Adcock, Market-Place, Aylesbury; Mr. Judd, Aylesbury Railway Station House; and of Mr. J. R. Gibbs, Walton-Street, Aylesbury.

The fare to Gravesend is 1s. each way. The admission to the Polytechnic Institution, and to the Zoological Gardens, is 1s. each. To the British Museum and National Gallery the public are admitted gratuitously, from ten till five.

N.B. In order that the necessary arrangements may be completed, parties are requested to make early application for tickets. After Saturday, the 22d of July, none will be issued.

ABOVE LEFT: An 1843 cheap excursion advertisement. (Hayward Parrott)

ABOVE RIGHT: George Carrington — on the commemorative railway medal of 1839. (Ralph May)

CENTRE: Mythical guardian of the railway reality: finial from the Railway Hotel roof. (County Museum)

BELOW: The mailman in 1902. (Ralph May)

ABOVE: Turning the first turf for the Metropolitan Railway May 5, 1892—
at Stoke Road. (Osterfield)

CENTRE: Death and disaster on the tracks, 1904.

BELOW: 1920 omnibus stand at Kingsbury Square: Young, and Cherry of
Waddesdon were among the first operators.

ABOVE LEFT: Oyez! The last time—Mr Slade, town crier.

ABOVE CENTRE: Louis XVIII. (Mansell Collection)

BELOW CENTRE: John Gibbs. (County Record Office)

ABOVE RIGHT: Admiral W. H. Smyth. (Margaret Sale)

CENTRE RIGHT: Baron Lionel Rothschild. (Mansell Collection)

BELOW RIGHT: J. Kersley Fowler.

My Lords, Ladies & Gentlemen

People make the place and Aylesbury has had its share of lords and ladies—and characters. Wilkes' memory died hard with Billy Guess (William Guest), who wore a cocked hat given to him by the politician, and died in 1834 at the ripe old age of 95—claiming he was 100. Two years later watchman Johnson carried a 20lb sack of beans a mile for a wager, and until his death in 1841, Jemmy Tucker would dress up at election times in a court dress, of cocked hat, light blue coat, embroidered waistcoat, satin breeches, low buckled shoes, frilled shirt, lace ruffles and a grand sash proclaiming his political loyalties.

In 1880 Frank Percy recalled a local legend: 'a local tradition, a tale very old; A legend of Aylesbury—a story retold.' This 'fragment of a credulous age' concerned a farmer and his dog. The farmer discovered a gap in one of his hedges that, however often he repaired it, was torn open afresh. He decided to wait for the culprit, 'squinny-eyed Dan,' with his 'Davy.' Night fell, and Dan came. The farmer's dog: 'Twas a savage great brute, black, shaggy and thin—Sagacious may be, but as ugly as sin!' confronted Dan. The next day both farmer and dog were found—dead. Dan was suspected but there was no evidence. Midnight came again, and Dan, drunk as a lord, danced on the dog's grave. Out of the ground rose the hound—'An omen of death calling Dan to his doom.' As it sank back into the ground, Dan fell, witless. He was found next, day babbling, taken home, and the constable called, but it was too late; he had died of fright.

In different literary vein, Admiral W. H. Smyth lived at St John's Lodge until his death in 1865. He was a descendant of Capt John Smith, coloniser of Virginia, and a gallant sailor in his youth. He wrote on matters historical, antiquarian and geographical, founded the Royal Geographical Society, of which he was sometime President, founded the United Services Institute and Museum, was President of the Astronomical Society, Vice-President of the Royal Society, a Director of the Society of Antiquities, and was associated with Greenwich Observatory.

Journalists such as the Gibbs gave much to Aylesbury: John, who founded the Aylesbury News, and Robert, whose history is the definitive work on the town. John was capable of a succinct turn of phrase. In a letter to the editor in 1857 he wrote, ending a quarrel by correspondence with the Rev Blackmore of Risborough, these words: 'argument with you is like arguing with a corkscrew.'

Disraeli visited, and once at Aylesbury, when a heckler called for him to speak 'louder and quicker' he replied: 'I am obliged to speak slowly to drive what I have to say into your thick head'. Said the heckler's companion 'You've got it now, Joe.'

Aylesbury has had its Royal residents too, not least the exiled Louis XVIII of France, who came with his court to Hartwell House in 1808. Homes in the neighbourhood were pressed into service for the courtiers—a cottage for the Duchesse d'Angouleme, a lodge for the Duc de Berri and another for the Duc de Blacas.

The French Queen died at Hartwell, and when Louis returned to his own land, he caused to be planted a garden at Versailles, modelled on the Queen's private garden at Hartwell, to commemorate 'the happy, happy days spent in that charming county.' Aylesbury went *en fete* in 1814 when Louis was restored, and Bourbon Street gained its name thus.

Louis' sojourn recalls the most famous of Aylesbury's Royal citizens—the Fair Maid of Aylesbury, Anne Boleyn. Her father was Lord of the Manor until he sold up to the Baldwins, saying then 'the truth is, that when I married my wife and I had but fifty pounds a year for me and my wife as long as my father lived, yet she brought me a child every year.' Of Anne, a contemporary wrote: 'that singular beauty and tendernesse'. So a humble daughter of an impoverished Aylesbury lord became queen of England and lost her head in more ways than one to Henry VIII. She was also the mother of Elizabeth I.

In a sense, the latterday lords of Aylesbury Vale, if not town, were the Rothschilds, Victorian bankers and entrepeneurs. In 1847 Baron Lionel, and his brothers Nathaniel, Anthony and Meyer came to the area. Their first association was through the stag hunting community. The Duke of Buckingham warned the hunting barons off his lands, and local farmers friendly to the newcomers offered them their fields, and released a stag at Broughton. The Rothschilds, perhaps encouraged by the warm welcome of the agricultural community, rapidly bought up property at Aston Clinton, Halton, Eythrope, Wing, Waddesdon and Wichendon. Baron Lionel built Waddesdon Manor—at a cost of £55,000 for the land, and £87,000 for the structure—the interior and fittings brought the outlay to some £2,000,000—plus. Baron Lionel thought it ought to be a good property at the price!

Perhaps the most famous and curious of characters was John Bigg. Clerk to Simon Mayne, regicide, he later became a recluse, living in a cave at Dinton, and living off local charity. He never changed his clothes, merely adding to them as they wore out by sewing on bits of this and that. He was said, without a shred of evidence, to have been Charles I's executioner, and was known as the Dinton Hermit.

Arguably, Aylesbury's most eccentric personality was Dr John Lee of Hartwell House. Lawyer, politician, Egyptologist and gentleman, he gained most notice for his astronomical work. He became a teetotaller, and a local benefactor. Many societies benefited from his generosity, as did sundry less deserving locals, who would live at his expense from his board, at no charge. He became an 'anti.' Not only anti-drink, he was against vaccination and a vegetarian. He even opposed religion. An eccentric in all things, he wore his hair long, such as it was, and wore a long blue coat with plain brass buttons, cravat and frilled shirt, dark trousers and beribboned shoes, the whole surmounted by a stove pipe hat. He married twice and ran the famous Gooseberry shows. His curious appearance was only matched by that of his drunken coachman Ben Monk.

Along the streets of memory file many more personalities, such as ebullient Mr Slade, last of the Town Criers; J. Kersley Fowler, farmer, publican and raconteur; artist/photographers Mr and Mrs Payne who caught the fleeting faces for posterity; Ivatts the shoemaker, whose shop still stands, and Pigeon Green a local 'street character'—merely a representative few of the people who have made the place.

ABOVE LEFT: John Bigg, the Dinton Hermit. (Margaret Sale)

ABOVE RIGHT: Anne Boleyn. (Mansell Collection)

BELOW: Dr Lee's residence — Hartwell House, 1860.

ABOVE LEFT: Pigeon Green, one of Aylesbury's early 20th century street characters. He would give his daily buttonhole to the first admiring lady. (Ralph May)

ABOVE RIGHT: Local models pose for Mr & Mrs Payne. (Ralph May)

BELOW LEFT: Shoemaker Ivatts. (Margaret Sale)

Good Old Days

The 19th century saw Aylesbury entering a period of poverty and change. The traditional crafts and farming were in serious decline, and the market was not what it had been. The political roisterings of centuries had been rationalised and calmed, and the town began to open up faster than ever before through the growing road, canal, and rail systems that punctuated the century. While the courts were long established and the gaol a disagreeable fact of life, few of the institutions of modern Aylesbury existed. The church still held sway over men's minds and souls, now in various creeds, and the town continued to be ruled by powerful men and vested interests. But this was to be challenged by the outside world, and by the growing unemployment.

In 1832 80 emigrants sailed from Wharf Yard en route to the States by way of Liverpool. In 1844 paupers from the Aylesbury Union were shipped off as emigrants. In 1845 soup kitchens distributed 1,000 quarts of soup to the poor at one time, arsonists were at work, and sheep stealing was rife.

At least two important institutions had been founded in previous centuries. Sir Henry Lee founded the original grammar school in the late 16th century with an endowment of £7 which he increased in 1598 and 1603.

The grammar school was built in 1714 by Henry Philips, who endowed it with £5,000. By 1806 the master's salary, which was subject to change at the whim of the trustees, was £60 per annum. The town hall had been 'much improved' by the turn of the century. In 1801 the population was 3,186. In 1801 the Pakingtons sold the Manor of Aylesbury to the Duke of Buckingham. Lord Carrington held the lease of the prebendal manor. Walton had been enclosed in 1799. And at Walton, the Coram Foundation had founded a foundlings hospital in 1674 with one hundred inmates.

By mid-century Aylesbury Hundred comprised 40,813 acres and 32 parishes lay within it. The population rose gradually to 3,447 in 1811 and then 4,400 in 1821 and ten years later to 4,907. In 1815 the rental value of property was put at £9,288, which made Aylesbury worth a good deal less than Chesham at £15,656; Chesham was also more populous.

The bounds of the manor were still being beaten in 1025 and each householder paid 1d as an acknowledgement of 'suit and service to the lord.' By contrast, the poor were numerous. In 1781 the contract for supplying and operating the Church-yard workhouse paid £669: William Foreman fulfilled it. By 1825 the payment per head was 4s 6d. In 1828 60 paupers complained to the magistrate about their pay. They were 'beyond all control, and nothing would satisfy them.' The workhouse was rebuilt in 1829 near Mount Street, later replaced by the Bierton Road building. In 1834 the inmates rioted. The Aylesbury Union House went up at Bierton Hill in 1844/5, and now forms part of Tindal General Hospital.

In 1827 there were proposals for a new infirmary, and in 1832 this was translated into fact by the conversion of an existing villa at the junction of Bicester and Buckingham roads. A 20 guinea subscription bought a life governorship, and a two guinea payment annual governorship. Subscribers had the gift of recommendation of patients, and one guinea subscribers could put up three out-patients; different payments warranted different quantities of patients through the subscriber. The doctors attended daily at 11 am to receive patients. 'No patients are admitted at any other time, except in case of accident or emergency . . . without a letter of recommendation.' An 'apparatus for the recovery of persons apparently drowned or suffocated etc., may be had by application at the Infirmary.' One hopes that the victims were close at hand. The year 1836/7 saw an income of £1,620 11s 2d. The balance in hand amounted to £2,592 7s 0d. In-patients in the year totalled 119, of whom 16 were already there. Four died, 52 were cured and 24 'relieved'. Two out-patients also died. In 1862 the new infirmary was opened.

Disaster was not confined to the inhabitants. On November 5, 1820 fire destroyed Wooton House, seat of Earl Temple in Bucks. An iron pipe (and not fireworks) was responsible, overheating (in the nursery) and catching the wainscoting. The house went up in 'one stupendous body of flame.' The loss was put at £40,000, and the building was uninsured. The Bucks Yeomanry attended all night, only to see the roof fall in at dawn.

Fire was an ever present hazard which the watchmen of Aylesbury had a first duty to guard against. In 1699 Walton experienced a major conflagration and in 1750 a fire started at a brick kiln near Cambridge Street, spreading rapidly to engulf the Dog and Duck on the site of the later Nag's Head, and between 30 and 40 thatched cottages, stables, outhouses and ricks to the tune of upwards of £1,600. This was followed fifteen years later by another disaster at The Crown. The Fire Brigade was taken over in 1830 by the local Board and by 1844 a fire engine and escape were available.

The original water supply in its wooden conduits was raised from 'the Friarage stream'; about 1733; it was eventually abandoned and later replaced in 1825 by water pumped by the prison treadmill from the Bear brook through iron pipes. This supply also ran dry after some years and when the prison was pulled down in 1846 ceased altogether. The town pump was put in in Kingsbury in 1838. In 1848 plans were laid for an artesian well, but the well was never sunk. It was not until 1858 that a serious proposal emerged for a waterworks, near Buckingham Street, raising water from Mill stream. The scheme failed. In 1865 the Chiltern Hills Water Co was formed, and in 1867 the works commenced pumping from Dancers End, Aston Clinton. The Kingsbury pump was removed in 1894.

In 1832 the cholera epidemic (250 cases; 50 dead) alerted the town to the need for improved sanitation and in 1842 a board succeeded the vestry to determine this and related matters. In 1848 an Inquiry led to the formation of the 1849 Board of Health, who considered the state of the town's drainage.

It took until 1870 to complete a sewerage system, when the Native Guano Company leased the sewage works.

Lighting exercised the townspeople perhaps as no other matter of public concern. By 1822 a few oil lamps were maintained, but in 1826 the town was still in virtual darkness. An Act was considered for public lighting, but there was soon an indication 'to shuffle out of the business.' Then followed meeting upon meeting—one was for going ahead despite the 'rabble' who opposed the proposals. In April 1829 the committee disintegrated for lack of cash and support, and the 'town is to recede into utter darkness, but which must lead to a flare up before long.' June saw a resurrection of interest, and in 1830 agreement coincided when the national act for the purpose was adopted locally and a Board of Lighting and Watching Inspectors elected. In 1834 a gas company was formed and the streets were duly lit up.

Throughout the century, Aylesbury saw a spate of public building. Although the Library Society existed in the 1820s, it was not until 1880 that the Reading Rooms were opened in Temple Street. Schools were spreading, with the British School opening at Green End in 1826, moving to the old workhouse building in 1830 (fees 2d per week). After a short closure, the school reopened in 1842, taking boys only until 1865 when girls were also admitted. In 1873 the premises were rebuilt.

The National Schools started in 1787 with the establishment of Sunday Schools; in 1826 a proper school was opened and in 1845 work started on buildings at Oxford Road, enlarged in 1870. St John's National School for infants was opened in 1856 at Bierton Road, and subsequently enlarged several times.

The clock tower which graces the Market Square succeeded an original clock on the 16th century old town hall, demolished in 1802, the intervening market house staying without one despite various proposals right up to its demolition in 1866. Today's tower was erected by public subscription in 1876.

In 1847 the Building Society was formed, and by 1887 there were five schools in the town apart from private schools. In 1895 the Public Baths were opened, and in 1889 the post office opened in High Street. The Victoria Club opened in Kingsbury in 1887, and the Aylesbury Co-operative Society was established in Silver Street in 1889. The Masonic Hall in Ripon Street was dedicated and opened in 1882.

The Isolation Hospital was opened at Stoke Mandeville in 1894 and Manor House Hospital was built in 1852. The Cemetery was established in 1857.

As the 19th century drew to a close, Aylesbury was no longer a purely market town. With growing industry, five schools, nine churches and its own Urban District Council, together with courts, county administration and extensive local services, it moved into modern times as a thriving and energetic community.

Change accelerated into the first half of the 20th century, with the Market Co selling the Town Hall to the Council in 1901 and a new Council Chamber opened in 1924. Five years later County Hall was completed, in Walton Street. Electricity came to Aylesbury in 1915, and the Cambridge Street fire station commenced operations in 1942. A telephone service started in 1901 and in 1921 tenants moved into the first six houses at the Southcourt estate. In 1938 the Market Square witnessed the last of the old pleasure fairs.

The Infirmary became the Royal Bucks Hospital, with numerous extensions and additions, and the Tindal House Poor Law Institution became a hospital, and was also much enlarged. Stoke Mandeville Hospital opened in 1940. The Isolation Hospital was enlarged in 1933 and became part of Stoke Mandeville in 1951. Manor House Hospital became a home for mentally handicapped children in 1928.

The old British School closed in 1907 and the National School at Walton in 1926. The Walton Road Grammar School was built in 1906, replacing the old Church Street premises, and was extended in 1931. Aylesbury Technical School opened in 1947; Queens Park County School in 1907, Southcourt County in 1926, Oak Green County in 1950, Tring Road County in 1948. St Mary's School was altered in 1931, and St John's School in 1925. The Public Baths closed in 1939 and the open air swimming pool opened in 1935.

ABOVE: Old Aylesbury. (County Record Office)

CENTRE: The old Grammar School. (Margaret Sale)

BELOW: Aylesbury Union Workhouse. (Bucks Reference Library)

Cambridge-Street, AYLESBURY.

TO BE SOLD BY AUCTION, BY MESSRS.

GIBBS AND SON

AT THE BLACK SWAN INN, AYLESBURY.

On FRIDAY, the 7th Day of NOVEMBER, 1851,

AT TWO O'CLOCK,—IN ONE LOT,

(*Subject to Conditions to be presented at the time of Sale,*)---*Those*

TWO COTTAGES,

IN CAMBRIDGE-STREET,

(Now unoccupied), adjoining the Blacksmith's-shop; they have each two rooms below, and two chambers, with a small yard behind.

The Cottages are Copyhold of the Manor of Bierton-with-Aylesbury. Fines very small.

POSSESSION MAY BE HAD THE TIME OF COMPLETING THE PURCHASE.

Further particulars may be known of the Auctioneers, Bourbon-street, Aylesbury.

R. Gibbs, Printer, Bourbon-street, opposite the Post-Office, Aylesbury.

ABOVE: Aylesbury Infirmary.

LEFT: Property sale, 1851. (Osterfield)

CENTRE RIGHT: Industry takes over: Bierton Lodge, demolished 1955 to make way for a jam factory. (E. D. Hollowday)

BELOW RIGHT: Late 18th century house in Ardenham Street. (Hayward Parrott)

A SCHOOL

WILL BE OPENED

On MONDAY Morning, the 6th of NOVEMBER,

IN THE OLD NATIONAL GIRLS' SCHOOL-ROOM,

FOR BOYS,

FROM FIVE TO FOURTEEN YEARS OLD.

This School will be conducted on Lancaster's or the Royal British Plan.

No Creed will be taught in this School, but the Children will learn to read the Scriptures without Note or Comment. Every Child will be required to go to the Sunday School to which his Parents belong.

The Charge will be Two-pence, per Week, to be paid to the Master.

The Boys must come to School with their Hair cut short, and their Faces and Hands clean.

Any Parent wishing his Children to be admitted into this School will apply to the Master, at the School Room, at Nine o'Clock on MONDAY MORNING NEXT, the 6th of NOVEMBER, or on any future Day (Sundays excepted) at the same Hour.

A SCHOOL FOR ADULTS

Will also be opened from the Hours of Six to Eight in the Evening.

Aylesbury, 3d of November, 1826.

BELOW: North front of the Museum, built 1718/19 for the Grammar School. (Hayward Parrott)

ABOVE: The British School opens its doors, 1826.
(Bucks Reference Library)

ABOVE LEFT: Mrs Dair's pupils, Bury House, Bicester Road, 1896.
(Margaret Sale)

CENTRE LEFT: The Victoria Club. (Bucks Reference Library)

BELOW LEFT: High Street as it once was. (County Record Office)

ABOVE RIGHT: The Public Baths.

CENTRE RIGHT: High Street junction with Market Square, turn of the
century. (Both Bucks Reference Library)

BELOW RIGHT: Walton Road before the car came.

ABOVE LEFT: Duck End, or Common Dunghill, looking towards Oxford Road before the Gatehouse estate was built. The cottages are believed to have been built by squatters around 1730. (Osterfield)

BELOW LEFT: Whitehall row. (Osterfield)

ABOVE CENTRE: Quiet Kingsbury, from Buckingham Road. (Ralph May)

BELOW CENTRE: Times begin to change — Bull's Head 'square' where there were twenty and more properties, long gone. (Both Margaret Sale)

ABOVE RIGHT: Edwardian Buckingham Street.

BELOW RIGHT: Silver Street, before Friar's Square took over.

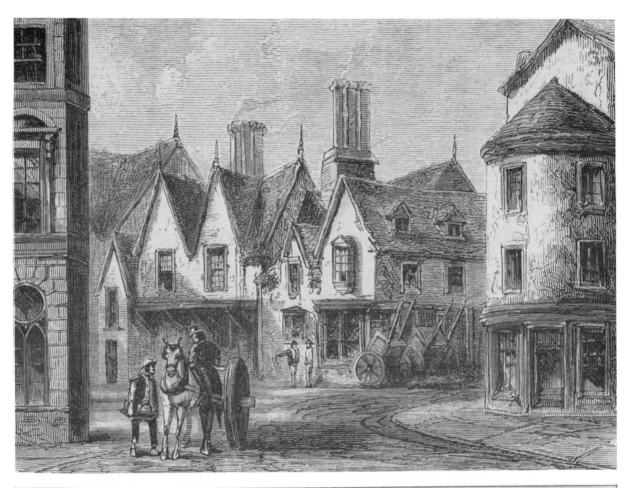

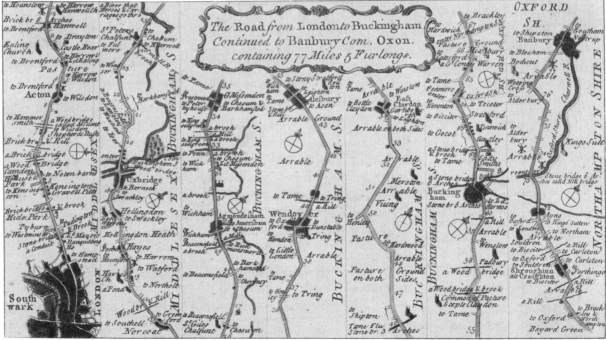

ABOVE: A last look at old Aylesbury: Kingsbury Square glimpsed beyond the original Round House.

BELOW: The raison d'etre behind the county town: an 18th century strip map shows the road from Buckingham to London — through Aylesbury.

Town for Today

In the last forty-five years, Aylesbury has changed more rapidly than ever before. The change is not only physical. The traditional character of the town has changed too, and some would say that it has lost its sense of history. Yet the town's heritage is still to be found in quiet squares and side streets, and a considerable variety of old, and some ancient buildings. Time lends perspective, and doubtless a future historian will chronicle the events of our century in relevant detail.

The main changes have been the population explosion to the present 60,000 and the remodelling of the town's centre with the monolithic County Hall, two shopping precincts, and demolition of the houses, shops and inns that formed the core of the town's old commercial, social and domestic life. The Market Square had become something of a vacuum in the midst of a one-way traffic system but in the 1990s traders returned; industry has chosen Aylesbury in considerable variety, bringing with it expanding employment and major expansion, particularly at Rabans Lane, while new office complexes stud the townscape at increasing intervals. While Stoke Mandeville has developed national status, and is scheduled for redevelopment, the 1862 Royal Bucks Hospital has closed. Its future remains uncertain.

Now two hypermarkets enhance Aylesbury's ancient role as a marketplace for the northern Chilterns and the Vale. Housing, both private and public, has mushroomed and local government has widened, though Aylesbury now returns but one member of Parliament.

Certainly, the farming community goes elsewhere for its markets, and the roads are perhaps less important than once they were, for no motorway straddles the county town as the old mail routes bisected it years ago, but the rail link with London has been revitalised with a quicker, cleaner Turbo service and new station facilities.

The ambitious remodelling of the town centre, with pedestrianisation, traditional street furniture and a £70 billion investment by Friends Provident, Unilever Superannuation and the District Council, has revolutionised the 1960s concrete Friars Square. In 1991 a horsed carriage visited Market Square for the first time in decades and the Cloisters opened where the '60s market once traded. The Council has spent £9 million on car parking since 1989 and British Rail put £79 million into the Chiltern Line which serves the town.

Between 1981 and 1991 Aylesbury's businesses increased by 58% and jobs went up from 49,200 to 60,000. Housing stock has increased to 22,900, from 16,000 in the late '70s. Population forecast for 2001 is 67,500. Complementing this commitment to growth, the county's Museum, in the heart of old Aylesbury, is undergoing a £3 million structural repair and refit, which includes a new Regional Art Gallery and the Roald Dahl Children's Gallery, to open again in 1994.

Aylesbury remains the hub of the Vale, and of the county, despite startling growth to the south, and the dynamic magnet of Milton Keynes to the north. It has reinforced its role as county town, extended its influence as the centre of a substantial local authority district, and attracted a considerable industrial presence. Accessible and prosperous, progressive and extrovert, it is perhaps a town more of the future than of the past, forging a new identity, and still changing.

LEFT: Old haunts new in Market Square (1975).

RIGHT: The Hale Leys Shopping Centre brings High Street and Market Square back into focus (1984).

BELOW: Rabans Lane industrial units march across the Vale, with CBS Manufacturing reflecting modern technology.

LEFT: Aylesbury Castle, seventies style.

RIGHT: The District Council complex maintains a low profile at 84, Walton Street.

CENTRE: The bland face of the Magistrates' Court off Walton Street.

BELOW: Its commercial days long gone, the canal basin harbours longboats for pleasure (1975).

ABOVE : The Market Square regains its traditional purpose (1993); BELOW : part
of Aylesbury's development — Watermead, on the Buckingham road.

LEFT : The Chiltern Line Turbo has brought London closer to the new-look
station; RIGHT : the Cloisters reflect major investment in Friars Square. BELOW :
Aylesbury's Museum approaches a new lease of life.

Bibliography

A History of Aylesbury by Robert Gibbs (Bucks Advertiser 1885).

County of Buckingham, Calendar to the Sessions Records (1678-1694 ed by William le Hardy, published by Guy R. Crouch, Clerk of the Peace, County Hall, under direction of the Standing Joint Committee of the Buckinghamshire Quarter Sessions and County Council, 1933 (Volume I).

As above, 1694-1705, ed by William le Hardy & Geoffrey Ll Reckitt. Pub. 1936 (Vol. II).

As above, 1705-1712 and appendix 1647, ed by Hardy and Reckitt. Published 1939 (Vol. III).

Records of Buckinghamshire, with transactions of the Architectural and Archaeological Society for the County of Buckingham, published by the Society, 1863 to date.

A History of the County of Buckingham, ed by William Page. The Victoria County History of the Counties of England (Constable & Co Ltd, 1905—Volume I).

Victoria History of the Counties of England: History of Buckinghamshire. Volume III, ed by William Page (1925).

The History and Antiquities of the County of Buckingham by George Lipscomb (Volume II) (J. & W. Robins, 1847).

Early Man in South Buckinghamshire by J. F. Head (John Wright & Sons, 1955).

The Episcopal Visittation Book, for the Archdeaconry of Buckingham 1662, ed E. R. C. Brinkworth (Buckinghamshire Record Society).

Ship Money Papers and Richard Grenville's Notebook, ed by Carol G. Bonsey and J. G. Jenkins (Record Society).

Subsidy Roll for the County of Buckingham, Anno 1524, ed Prof A. C. Chibnall and A. Vere Woodman (Record Society).

The Certificate of Musters for Buckinghamshire in 1522, ed by A. C. Chibnall (Record Society).

The Signatories of the Orthodox Confession of 1679 by Arnold H. J. Baines (The Carey Kingsgate Press Ltd, 1960).

Aylesbury in the Fifteenth Century, A Bailiff's Notebook, by Elizabeth M. Elvey, MA.

Annals of Aylesbury 1882-1952 by Hayward Parrott (R. May 1952).

Magna Britannica by Rev Daniel Lysons, 1806.

Britannia by W. Camden, 1771.

Leland's Itinerary.

Pigot & Co's Directory of Buckinghamshire, 1823.

Directory of Bucks: Musson & Craven, 1853.

Kelly's Directory for Buckinghamshire, 1899.

Kelly's Directory of Aylesbury and Stoke Mandeville, 1974.

An Aylesbury Diary 1821-1848.

Records of Old Times by J. Kersley Fowler (Chatto & Windus 1898).

Echoes of Old County Life by Fowler (Edward Arnold 1892).

Recollections of Old Country Life by Fowler (Longmans Green & Co 1894).

Old Works and Past Days in Rural Buckinghamshire by G. Eland (G. T. de Fraine & Co Ltd, 1921).

Index

Index Additions